CURRENT NATIONAL BIBLIOGRAPHIES
OF LATIN AMERICA

CURRENT NATIONAL BIBLIOGRAPHIES OF LATIN AMERICA
A State of the Art Study

Irene Zimmerman

Center for Latin American Studies
University of Florida / 1971
Gainesville

A Center for Latin American Studies Publication

Library of Congress
Catalog Card No. 73-632969
ISBN 0-8130-0321-0

PRINTED IN FLORIDA

PREFACE

THIS ACCOUNT of the "state of the art" of national bibliography in the component countries and regions of "Latin America," broadly interpreted, was undertaken partially as a result of the author's participation in the lengthening series of Seminars on the Acquisition of Latin American Library Materials (SALALM), which have been held annually from June 1956.

Since knowledge of what exists is prerequisite to securing it, information as to what publications have been produced has necessarily been a concern of the Seminars, and a Committee on Bibliography was soon established. This writer has served on the Committee throughout its existence and was for a time chairman of a Subcommittee on Caribbean Bibliography. Some time ago a suggestion was made that the Committee on Bibliography might well undertake to update the working papers on national bibliography which had been contributed at successive Seminars. Such an undertaking did not seem feasible as a committee project, but the need was recognized.

Consequently, when the opportunity arose to apply for a Faculty Development Grant which would provide a quarter's leave from regular duties, it was decided to do so in order to undertake the present study. The time specified was the spring quarter of 1969, March 15 to June 15.

v

Obviously one quarter was a very short time to devote to such a study, but the favorable factors included a reasonably good acquaintance with the subject and a fortunate coincidence. A colleague, Mrs. Rosa Quintero Mesa, had for several years been engaged in a major cooperative bibliographic project—the preparation of a set of volumes covering the official serial publications of the twenty Latin American republics. Since these would normally include whatever data were being provided by a given country about its own current national bibliography, a valuable source of information was close at hand. A trip made by Mrs. Mesa early in 1969 to the west coast countries of South America and to the two inland countries, Bolivia and Paraguay, for the procurement of documents gave further assurance of updated information.

The fact that her itinerary covered the area it did was a further helpful coincidence. It enabled the author to devote the one month's trip (which was made possible by a travel grant from the University of Florida's Center for Latin American Studies) to the east coast countries and Chile. In all of those countries more information was needed than was furnished in the latest available publications. The visit was the more important because a stated secondary objective of the quarter's leave was to learn as much as possible about the bibliographical coverage of social science fields, such as education, economics, and law, on a comprehensive Latin American basis. That topic, however, has necessarily been left for possible treatment at a later date. Mexico and Central America could not be visited at this time, but the writer was reasonably well acquainted with the area, and the situations there seemed reasonably clear.

The Caribbean area, in which some of the most exciting developments were taking place, is the writer's field of special interest. By another fortunate coincidence the Fourteenth Seminar was to be held in Puerto Rico in June, just as she would be returning from the quarter's leave. The fact that two additional conferences, devoted specifically to Caribbean matters, would be held in the Virgin Islands and Puerto Rico at the beginning and at the end of the quarter, respectively, could not have been anticipated, but in that area where events are moving so rapidly and where bibliographical matters of great promise are in a state of crisis at present, the development was helpful.

The one disadvantage in the series of conferences, so far as the present project was concerned, was that the time required for preparation, attendance, and follow-up of each made it impossible to present even an outline of findings concerning the current national bibliographies of Latin America within the allotted quarter's leave. Consequently, this study has had to be prepared in the limited amount of time which has been available since returning to a full work schedule. In a few instances further correspondence or procurement of materials would have been advantageous, but since timeliness in a project such as this is a major consideration, it has seemed best to conclude it on the basis of present information, with apologies for whatever deficiencies or oversights may be found to exist.

It is impossible to acknowledge adequately the assistance and encouragement given by a great many people, help without which this study would not have been written. The cooperation in person of members of the book world in South America and the Caribbean, and elsewhere through correspondence, is greatly appreciated. Credit is implicitly given to a number of persons in the course of the study. It should be made explicit in a few instances, beginning with Marietta Daniels Shepard, the chief founder and the moving spirit of the Seminars on the Acquisition of Latin American Library Materials, the circles of whose influence seem ever widening. The urging on of a flagging spirit by Mrs. M. J. Savary, who visited Gainesville at a critical time, was a decisive factor. The reading of an early portion of the manuscript by William V. Jackson and his later encouragement are appreciated. Finally, the suggestions made by an assistant, Mrs. Sammy Alzofon Kinard, who has cheerfully read the entire manuscript, have been most helpful, as has been also her assistance with technical details. Needless to say, the sole responsibility for all defects is exclusively mine.

Irene Zimmerman

January 1970

CONTENTS

CONTENTS

I

INTRODUCTION

THE FIRST OBJECTIVE of this "state of the art" study of the current national bibliographies of Latin America is to indicate the status of the chief published sources of information about the current production of book materials in each of the countries concerned. Since bibliography is compiled rather than written, it might seem to the uninitiated a purely mechanical matter to assemble the necessary information, to arrange it as desired, and to send it to the printer or publisher. It is true that, given an ordinary book, a person with minimal training can jot down the author, title, place and date of publication, publisher, and number of pages, and so can produce a completed entry. If these data are not all available in the most obvious places, or if there is additional information to note, such as the fact that the book is one of a series, somewhat longer will be required.

This situation presupposes several things—that the book is at hand, that it is sufficiently well organized to show the expected data, and that the person handling the item has enough training to recognize and list the information correctly and in usable form. If it is expected that any analysis or noting of contents is to be done, a corresponding increase in the qualifications of the bibliographer is of course required. The first supposition, that books produced in a country are all collected in some one place and await recording, is a hazardous one in most countries, and in all

1

Latin American countries it is completely false. One is reminded of the old recipe for Welsh rarebit, which began: "First catch your hare." It is also hazardous to assume that once the bibliographer has succeeded in assembling the information, it will necessarily be published. Too often the potential publisher and the possible purchaser seem to think primarily in terms of paper and ink—that a book is a book is a book—and that the price should be based mainly on the number of pages.

In any country the preparation and production of a list of the publications currently issued by its presses is a unique story. It is the state of the art of national bibliography in the various Latin American countries which is the subject of the present study. This involves not a mere listing of sources which tell something about the publications of each country nor even an annotated bibliography describing them. It requires an attempt to describe the major characteristics of each individual situation and the results of whatever efforts are being made to produce a current record of a given country's publications.

The state of the art of any national bibliography is the product of many variables. These can produce surprising results. Some of the larger countries have so far provided only woefully incomplete records of their national book production. On the other hand, there are small countries whose records are excellent. It is these differing conditions that lend interest and significance to a country-by-country analysis of the matter. This study will attempt to describe—so far as this non-Latin but nonpartisan and interested observer can do from the facts at hand—the situation as it exists in each country, or, in present terms, the state of the art in each.

We have been accustomed to use the term "Latin American" to refer to the twenty countries in the Western Hemisphere whose official language is Spanish, Portuguese, or French. For present purposes the Commonwealth of Puerto Rico and the new English-speaking countries of the Caribbean area must also be at least summarily considered. This would be necessary if only because three of the latter—Barbados, Jamaica, and Trinidad and Tobago—have become members of the Organization of American States, while Guyana (which has not yet elected to join the OAS) is a part of the South American continent. In addition there are significant and promising developments on a regional basis which include all these political entities and without which any consideration of the Caribbean area would be unrealistic.

Of reference tools produced in the Americas which deal specifically with *current* Latin American publications, only the *Handbook of Latin American Studies* is sufficiently broad to include all the countries and areas to be considered here. The *Handbook* is of course a subject bibliography. It includes current materials *about* Latin America, wherever published, arranged by subject rather than by place of origin. Consequently, its value as a source of information about a given country's current publications, as such, is very limited. There are other important reference tools, such as catalogs of Latin American collections or acquisitions lists, whose value as sources of current Latin American bibliography is in inverse ratio to their breadth of scope and their depth in time. However, there are a few which deal sufficiently with current publications from specific portions of Latin America to merit consideration in their proper places.

Once the facts and situations concerning Latin America as a whole have been presented, the countries will be divided into two groups: (1) the ten Spanish- or Portuguese-speaking republics of South America, and (2) the "Caribbean area" with the term used to include Mexico, Central America, and the Antilles.

The term "national bibliography" is a comprehensive one. Ordinarily, publications to be considered as registers of their country's publications will be bulletins or annuals devoted to a presumably inclusive listing of at least the books and pamphlets published in a country during a stated time period. If the records include periodicals, government documents, theses, and whatever else a printing press (or in some cases a mimeograph) can produce, so much the better. In exceptional cases, if basic information has been consistently provided in some specific journal or review rather than in a bulletin devoted exclusively to bibliography, the fact may be mentioned. Commercial records covering more than one country will be considered on their merits. If there is nothing to report, so be it.

Inherent in the question of the state of the art is the qualitative one—to what extent are techniques employed which make the end product acceptable? For twenty years or more the Pan American Union and UNESCO have been working to upgrade the bibliographic patterns used in Latin America to insure that "bibliographies" will provide full and exact citations, including such details as the full and correct name of an author, the place and date of publication, and the extent of the item cited.

Now, as we enter the seventies, most of the volunteer UNESCO -inspired *grupos bibliográficos* have faded away. In some cases the result is a total vacuum. If the country is one where there is minimal compliance with a toothless law of legal deposit, that fact is an integral part of the picture. In the course of this study questions may be raised which lie beyond its scope to consider in detail, for instance, "To what extent are libraries—national or otherwise—looked upon primarily as book repositories rather than as centers of study and research?" or "What is the relationship between such situations and attitudes towards librarians and bibliographers?" They should be kept in mind, however, as they bear directly upon the possibilities of developing adequate national or other bibliographies.

This study cannot go into detail on all possible questions for any one country, but situations described in one country may be directly relevant to those of another. The fact is illustrated by a recent report resulting from a foundation-financed study by two eminent librarians.* *The Mexican Library* by Paul Bixler, published in 1969 by the Scarecrow Press, raises questions similar to those posed above and others which may well be kept in mind in the consideration of situations in the various countries. To what extent is there cooperation and interaction between the library world and book publisher and dealer? If libraries are looked upon chiefly as would-be recipients of free books rather than as customers and colleagues, how can the situation and the "image" be altered? To what extent is the librarian equipped to handle present responsibilities? How can he gain support for needed improvements?

The new decade should bring some helpful answers to these and similar questions. Cumulative effects of various national and international efforts are visible, for instance, in the increasing number and vigor of national bibliographic institutes and departments of library science. As the decade opens, Latin America's second graduate school of library science begins its first full year in fine new quarters, the bicultural setting of the University of Puerto Rico. It is in Puerto Rico also, where the Caribbean Regional Library was left in trust to the Commonwealth by the expiring Caribbean Organization in 1964, that a regional bibliography is being compiled, using modern computerized methods. In Argentina colleagues in the University of Buenos Aires, experts respectively in bibliography and in computerization, have a proposal which could bypass the roadblock of an inert national library. In Brazil the organized book trade is working actively with representatives of the library world to improve information provided to the public concerning the country's current book production. Such factors are an important part of the current scene in Latin America. They bear directly upon the state of the national bibliography of the various countries and will be considered in connection with it.

To consider the negative side for a moment, this study will not attempt

* Carl M. White's report is *Mexico's Library and Information Services: a Study of Present Conditions and Needs.* It was published by the Bedminster Press, Totowa, New Jersey, in 1969, too late to be available for purposes of the present study, unfortunately.

to answer the question, "Where can we find any information at all that would be helpful in acquiring books from Latin America?" Such inquiries may be referred to a paper presented by Carl W. Deal to the Twelfth Seminar on the Acquisition of Latin American Library Materials (1967), "Bibliographic Aids for Collecting Latin American Materials." Also, the 1969 edition of the Fermín Peraza *Bibliografías corrientes de la América Latina* is even more comprehensive than earlier ones and includes much information about partial sources of national bibliography.

Sources of information cited, other than national publications specifically devoted to bibliography, will be limited, with one exception, to works published in the Americas. An exception must be made in the case of UNESCO, whose efforts to promote the development of national bibliography in the Americas (as elsewhere) date from the historic Conference on the Improvement of Bibliographical Services held in 1950 at UNESCO headquarters in Paris. Because of the special needs of Latin America and requests from it, a Regional Center for the Western Hemisphere was established with headquarters in Havana. During the fifties much groundwork was laid and an active campaign was waged for the initiation and improvement of national bibliography. Inspiration and leadership were provided, especially by the Argentine-born Carlos Víctor Penna, the Center's Assistant Director for Cultural Affairs. Numerous national and international seminars provided opportunity for a sharing of information, experiences, and ideas, and incidentally for leadership training. Although events in Cuba since 1959 have made the Western Hemisphere Center relatively inactive, the Paris office of UNESCO has continued to give all possible assistance to Latin America.

An early and major contribution of UNESCO was its bibliographic handbook, *Bibliographical Services Throughout the World,* of which the first edition covered 1951-1953 and the second 1950-1959. A third edition, covering 1960-1964, was published in French in 1967. An English edition was advertised for the following year, but as of mid-1969 it was reported not yet available. Unfortunately much of its value is already lost, but the information is being updated, a few countries at a time, in the monthly issues of the UNESCO bulletin, *Bibliography, Documentation, and Terminology.* These have been consulted to ascertain which Latin American countries have been covered, and reference will be made to data from the bulletin where appropriate.

Of publications originating in the United States the most important for present purposes are the relevant working papers prepared for the annual

Seminars on the Acquisition of Latin American Library Materials from 1956 to date. (The Seminars were originally sponsored by the Pan American Union, but they were formally incorporated in 1968 under the acronym SALALM.*) By 1966 the national bibliographies of all countries were presumably covered, so far as possible, by reports from their own nationals. Of the major countries only Peru was not represented. For some of the smaller countries there was and is, unfortunately, no reliable source of information about whatever publishing may be done there. In such cases the situation can only be described as it appears to exist. An annual SALALM working paper devoted to bibliographic activities for the past year makes a point of providing information on developments concerning current national bibliography. Hereafter in this study each Seminar will be identified only by its number and year, though the acronym will be frequently used.

Two periodical publications of the Pan American Union are useful. The quarterly *Inter-American Review of Bibliography* has a notes-and-news section arranged by countries, and "Recent Books" includes a listing on bibliography. *The List of Books Accessioned and Periodical Articles Indexed,* published monthly by the Pan American Union's Columbus Memorial Library, devotes sections in both categories to bibliography and may be depended upon to note items concerning national bibliography.

The *Handbook of Latin American Studies,* prepared at the Library of Congress by its Hispanic Foundation, provides an annual annotated section, "Bibliography," which is most helpful. In 1964, the same year that this special section was reinstated, the *Handbook* began to devote alternate years to the humanities and to the social sciences. The division fortunately does not apply to bibliography. The *Handbook* also presents occasional special articles on national bibliography, such as a general one in 1960 on "Records of Current Publishing in Latin America" by Helen F. Conover, with descriptive annotations by Peter de la Garza. Later and more specific articles will be cited in their appropriate context. Despite its being a subject bibliography, the *Handbook*'s regional subdivisions and a subject index do give it a limited value as a country approach, especially for countries where national bibliography is lacking or scarce.

In the present paper, which focuses on current situations, minimal attention can be given to bibliographic history or to such marginal publications as periodicals or reviews which include a bibliographic section. Information concerning such publications is already available from other sources.

* For further information and a list of the Seminars, see Appendix.

Fermín Peraza's *Bibliografías corrientes de la América Latina* has been published in successive editions since 1962. The sixth edition had been completed before death claimed Dr. Peraza on January 31, 1969, and it is available from his widow.* It provides full bibliographic data about the 236 items listed. These include, for instance, general publications with only a section devoted to Latin America and bulletins dealing with specialized aspects of national bibliography, which lie beyond the scope of the present study. Contents notes are frequently included.

Two works dealing with Latin American bibliography and including sections on national bibliography are invaluable for retrospective background. *Obras de referencia de América Latina*, by Abel Rodolfo Geoghegan, which was subsidized by UNESCO and published in Buenos Aires in 1965 by the compiler, includes sections on the current national bibliographies of the various countries as of that date. A *Bibliography of Latin American Bibliographies*, by Arthur E. Gropp, Director Emeritus of the Columbus Memorial Library, was published in 1968. It lists 224 items under "Bibliografía nacional." For titles having open entries, the date of the latest volume received at the Pan American Union may be given. However, all items, including last minute insertions, have imprint dates prior to January 1, 1965.

Periodicals are always an important part of the printed record, but for underdeveloped countries, where publications of books and pamphlets is minimal, they are especially so. However, they are frequently ignored in records of national bibliography if—as is often the case with official publications also—they are not subject to requirements for legal deposit. It remains true that the only comparatively recent attempt to treat Latin American periodicals on a national basis is the highly selective *Guide to Current Latin American Periodicals* by Irene Zimmerman, published in 1961. Besides annotations for individual titles, the introduction for each country noted important serials which provided significant information about the national bibliography.

Although its only national approach is on a subject basis, mention should be made of an important quarterly index which has been prepared since 1961 by Jorge Grossmann at the Library of the Pan American Union: *Indice general de publicaciones periódicas latinoamericanas: humanidades y ciencias sociales. Index to Latin American Periodicals: Humanities and Social Sciences.* (The original publisher, G. K. Hall, was superseded by the Scarecrow Press, beginning with the 1963 volume.) Each of the first three

* Elena V. Peraza, P.O. Box 9177, University of Miami Branch, Coral Gables, Florida 33124.

quarterly issues has an author index. The fourth is a cumulated issue, which may be considerably delayed in appearing.

Official government publications represent an important part of the national production of book materials, but they are in general a neglected one. For some Latin American countries, if not most, the series compiled in the late 1940s at the Library of Congress, *A Guide to the Official Publications of the Other American Republics* (1945-1949) under the general editorship of James B. Childs, still stands as the best record of such publications.

Following a discussion at the Sixth Seminar (1961) of the need for more adequate bibliographies of Latin American serial documents, Stanley L. West, who was then the Director of the University of Florida Libraries, agreed to explore possibilities. What was to become a major cooperative enterprise was instituted by the Libraries' Documents Department. Mrs. Rosa Q. Mesa was employed to undertake the task of compiling data for representative countries, based on basic bibliographies and the University of Florida's holdings. At the Eighth Seminar (1963) results for three countries were presented and discussed. Florida was officially requested to continue with and to develop the project to include all of the Latin American republics. It agreed to do so if outside financial support could be secured. A grant from the Ford Foundation, approved in December 1964, made possible the expanded program. As a result, the lists as compiled from available sources were checked against the holdings of the Library of Congress and the New York Public Library and of those university libraries with Farmington Plan or other strong specialization in a specific area.

The series, "Latin American Serial Documents," is being published by University Microfilms-Xerox. By late 1969 the volumes for Colombia, Brazil, and Cuba had appeared. Mexico is next in order, after which the remaining eight volumes for South American countries will follow in alphabetical order. The Dominican Republic and Haiti will share the succeeding volume, after which the Central American republics, again in alphabetical order, will conclude the series. Inasmuch as the great majority of educational and cultural institutions in Latin America are financed by the national governments, the term "official" was interpreted liberally enough to include many of the institutions' serial publications, thereby greatly increasing the bibliographic value of the lists.

Since the closing date was December 1966 and the project is not a continuing one, the inclusion of the series here might be questioned. Justification lies in the fact that, in general, official documents are inadequately recorded in most Latin American countries. These new lists provide data hitherto unavailable in many of them, and also provide a working basis upon which it is hoped the countries can and will build. The state of the art would be greatly advanced by the improvement of that basic starting point, government organization manuals, in the countries where they exist and by their initiation in the too great number where they are now lacking.

Among the promising developments of the past decade have been improvements in the methods of the commercial book trade for the supplying of Latin American book materials to the United States market and the more or less incidental increase in the bibliographical information provided by dealers and publishers. It is apparent that the example of firms based in the United States—and perhaps their competition—have led to instances, at least, of improved practices in individual Latin American countries. However, our concern here is with the overall picture.

The Latin American Cooperative Acquisition Program, commonly known as LACAP, is the response of Stechert-Hafner ("The World's Leading International Booksellers") to the needs of university libraries, as that program has developed from 1960, when the Fifth Seminar convened at the New York Public Library. At that meeting, memorable in many respects, Nettie Lee Benson, dynamic librarian in charge of the Latin American Collection of the University of Texas, who had been inveigled by Stechert-Hafner into making an exploratory and book-buying trip to South America, gave a graphic report on the book trade as she had found it (Special report no. 1). The resulting story has been told by M. J. Savary in *The Latin American Cooperative Acquisitions Program, an Imaginative Venture* (1968) and need not be related here.

For present purposes our concern is with the nature and extent of bibliographic information regarding current publications which is made available through the LACAP catalog. Beginning in 1960, Stechert-Hafner began to issue a special series of numbered lists under the general title *New Latin American Books: An Advance Checklist of Newly Published Titles Just Acquired under the Latin American Cooperative Acquisitions Project (LACAP).* These lists, devoted entirely to recently published titles from one or more countries or areas, provide a great deal of information. In some cases it may be available from national sources at about the same time. In others, notably in many of the smaller countries, neither catalogs nor bibliographies provide the information early or late.

The lists are designed, admittedly, as booksellers' instruments rather than as bibliographic aids. However, their usefulness as selection tools, as well as for later reference use, would be enhanced by fuller bibliographic data, notably publisher and number of pages, as well as series and edition, now usually given when applicable. As the lists stand, with incomplete data and no cumulative indexing, their bibliographic value is minimal, but it is not altogether negligible.

The success of the Stechert-Hafner LACAP program has led to the offering of "general order" programs by other dealers. Outstanding among these is Fernando García Cambeiro, of Buenos Aires. He offers an "ABC plan," designed to provide institutional customers with selected materials from a country or region of its choice or on specific topics. He has published three times a year since about 1964 a *Monthly News Service* catalog which lists Argentine publications on a classified basis, with no index. Bibliographic data for these Argentine lists include publisher, paging, and series. However, for the *Suplementos latinoamericanos*, which list publications from elsewhere, by country, the range of bibliographic data is from good to poor. It is sometimes subminimal, providing only surname, title, place, date, and price.

One of the participants in the Fifth Seminar was Daniel Melcher, then Executive Director of the R. R. Bowker Company. He heard the report of Nettie Lee Benson on the difficulties and the hazards of the book trade in Latin America. The challenge to the veteran bookman was irresistible. He undertook to wager the R. R. Bowker Company's experience that publications comparable to *Publishers' Weekly* and to *Books in Print* would render such a major service that they would prove commercially viable. SALALM participants applauded, but there were doubters as to the feasibility of the Bowker undertaking. However, a beginning was made when Robert Kingery, representing the New York Public Library, agreed that if a subsidy could be provided to cover expenses, the numerous materials coming into the New York Public Library from all parts of Spanish America and the corresponding invoices could be made available for the Bowker experiment.

In October 1961 the R. R. Bowker Company proudly presented the first issue of its quarterly bulletin, *Fichero bibliográfico hispanoamericano: catálogo de toda clase de libros publicados en las Américas en español* (thus eliminating by definition Brazil and Haiti). For three years *Fichero* was prepared at the New York Public Library by two skilled cataloguers, Abel Rodolfo Geoghegan of Argentina and Mrs. María Elena Cardona of Nicaraguan origin. The combination of a supply of materials greater than existed at any one spot in Latin America and of technical skill—subsidized initially by the Rockefeller Foundation—produced an excellent and valuable tool.

When the subsidy expired, *Fichero*, with the prestige of three successful years behind it, was transplanted to Buenos Aires, the major publishing center of Latin America. Under the direction of Mary C. Turner, a long-time member of the New York staff, the youthful experiment survived, but it necessarily adapted itself to its new environment. Without the continuous book flow from Spanish American countries to the Acquisitions Department of the great New York Public Library, and in a professional and cultural atmosphere more oriented toward Europe than toward the other American republics, *Fichero* underwent major changes. It became a monthly rather than a quarterly periodical. No longer a professed "catalog of every kind of book published in the Americas in Spanish," it became one listing books published in the Spanish language in the Americas and in Spain.

The present *Fichero bibliográfico hispanoamericano* carries no qualifying subtitle. However, an orientation toward Spain was implicit in an article in the issue for October 1968, "Bibliografías corrientes de libros en nuestro idioma," in which the editor listed and commented upon "useful" periodicals and catalogs from Latin America and from Spain. Further evidence of the orientation is seen in the relative number of firms and institutions listed in three consecutive numbers (March-June 1969) as ones whose publications were listed in them. Of a total of 319, the number from Spain was 76, or 24 percent. The 26 percent from Argentina and 22 percent from Mexico left a remainder of only 28 percent from all the rest of Spanish America. It is in the potential expansion of the 28 percent to represent countries other than the two major publishing centers of Spanish America that the possible future of *Fichero bibliográfico hispanoamericano* as a really valuable Spanish American bibliographical tool lies. This is a matter of education and persuasion.

For particular instance, Chile and Peru have been among the countries most poorly represented in *Fichero*. The recent concession made by the Chilean publisher and dealer, Sr. Zamorano y Caperán, who agreed to include the names of publishers in his bimonthly *Servicio bibliográfico chileno*, should remedy the lack of Chilean representation. The cooperation of E. Iturriaga & Cía., S.A., of Lima, whose semiannual *Libros recientes* already includes full bibliographic data, would, by supplying his lists to *Fichero*, improve the information it now makes available concerning Peruvian publications.

For the smaller countries, in many of which no publishers' or dealers' catalogs are regularly produced, the provision by the Stechert-Hafner LACAP lists of data as to publishers would not only add information of importance to their potential customers but would also, by making possible the inclusion of the items in *Fichero*, expand considerably the world's scanty knowledge of such publishing as is being done in those countries. The promise made to the Fourteenth Seminar (1969) by Dominick Coppola, a regular participant in SALALM and now the president of the Stechert-Hafner firm, to consider the matter seriously, lends hope that this additional cooperation between dealer and publisher may be extended. The evidence is that it would work to their mutual benefit as well as contribute to the improvement of bibliographical tools.

Fichero bibliográfico hispanoamericano is, as matters now stand, a monthly trade bulletin of some seventy pages, published by Bowker Editores Argentina, S.A. Its reason for existence is to provide a listing, arranged by the Dewey Decimal System, of books and pamphlets recently published in Spanish-speaking countries. Bibliographic data are apparently full when they are taken from publications made available to the office, and otherwise are as full as the publisher provides. Prices are stated in the currency of the country of publication. Numerous advertisements and occasional articles are included. Indexing consists of a table of contents by classification, an author index, a title index, and an alphabetical list of publishers. Its usefulness is limited by its noninclusiveness, but it seems our present best hope for a bibliographic tool of hemispheric scope.

When Daniel Melcher spoke to an approving SALALM audience in 1960, his vision of possibilities was expressed in terms of a volume comparable in nature to *Books in Print*. Quite possibly he considered the publication of a bibliographic bulletin such as *Fichero* primarily as an intermediate step. For the next four years SALALM was given occasional progress reports. Uncertainty as to title was resolved in favor of *Libros en venta*, in view of the hazards of stating that books were actually "in print" but hoping that a reasonably large proportion of them would be "for sale," as reported by their publishers.

The appearance in 1964 of *Libros en venta en Hispanoamérica y España* was a major event. By the time it was printed, of course, many of the books listed as "for sale" were, in the fantastically short-lived book markets of Latin America, no longer available, and many new titles had taken their places on the shelves. However, the appearance of *Libros en venta* represented two major achievements: (1) more or less complete bibliographical information had been provided concerning a sizable portion of the book production of Spanish America, much of which would not have been registered otherwise; and (2) information was available both on a classified basis and by author and title. Also, a price was usually given.

Even though the price might not still be effective, it would serve the dual purpose of indicating the value placed upon the book by the publisher as of that date and of providing persons who might wish to order the book with a specific detail often insisted upon by acquisitions departments (which are quite properly wary of blank-check procedures).

Justification of the inclusion of *Libros en venta* in a study devoted to the state of "current" bibliography lies in the supplements which have so far appeared and which can, we hope, be expected at two-year intervals. A *Suplemento* for 1964/1966 was published late in 1967. Early in 1969 *Fichero* announced that a supplement covering books produced in Spanish during the years 1967 and 1968 was being compiled. Publishers were asked to submit updated lists of new titles and revised editions published during those years.*

If, in fact, biennial cumulated lists of an increasing portion of even the books and pamphlets produced by commercial firms and by non-governmental organizations during those two years can be made available, the benefits will be great. The first advantages would fall properly to the publishers and the authors represented, in that they would be encouraged to keep their wares available in anticipation of new orders. Bibliographers would benefit, whether in the interests of acquisitions or of research projects, by having the data available. And in specific terms of this study, the countries which have the most inadequate records themselves would have available quantities of information from which it would be possible to extract data, it is hoped by computer, to provide those countries with more nearly current national bibliography than anything now at their disposal. Obviously, the better the bibliographic quality of the data provided, the better the potentialities for any compilations based upon them.

In general, then, this publishing enterprise of Bowker Editores Argentina, S.A., may be said to constitute the only major organized and reasonably well-established attempt to provide a regional bibliography covering Spanish America, but also including Spain.

From the point of view of the researcher the inclusion of peninsular publications has both advantages and disadvantages. Although it increases the bulk of potentially nonrelevant items listed, the comprehensive coverage obviates the necessity of considering, for instance, at what point a Spanish émigré became more properly a Mexican or a Venezuelan author than a Spanish one.

---

* The 1967/1968 *Suplemento* was completed late in 1969. Copies for distribution in the United States were shipped to the R. R. Bowker Company about the middle of December. (Letter from Mary C. Turner, March 5, 1970.)

The noninclusion of Brazilian and Haitian materials in *Fichero* and *Libros en venta* will presumably continue. Brazil, with its half-a-continent expanse and its Portuguese language, has its own special orientations and problems. It has also imaginative, well-informed, and enterprising personnel in publishing, bibliography, and library fields who are able and willing to benefit from both American and European experience and from whom real advances in the state of Brazilian national bibliography may be expected. Haiti—poor, beautiful French- (and Creole-) speaking Haiti—has at this point little to contribute to or little to gain from a fully "Latin American" bibliography.

Comentarios bibliográficos americanos, a new venture, is too young to assess adequately, but one fact stands out. This striking, colorful, and human-interest attempt to provide bibliographical coverage of Latin American book production is in marked contrast to *Fichero* and *Libros en venta* (whose success may depend largely upon how well their editor succeeds in adapting the sophisticated computerized techniques of the parent R. R. Bowker Company to their own needs). The first issue of *Comentarios bibliográficos americanos* was dated as a quarterly, January/March 1969. However, it announced itself as a bimonthly, with an annual cumulated catalog available on separate subscription.* The basic arrangement is by the Dewey Decimal System, with an alphabetical key provided, as are also a table of contents, an author index, and a list of publishers. There is no general introduction, but scattered notes indicate that the CBA considers itself primarily a cultural enterprise. This was also the impression gained from a brief interview with the editor, Eduardo Darino.†

The "commentaries" in *Comentarios bibliográficos americanos* provide, besides occasional annotations on books listed, news notes about contests and prizes, best-seller lists in Uruguay and Argentina, and other items. The *CBA* staff includes, besides the office personnel, a list of research assistants from six countries and a number of consultants—professors or others—for various fields. Promotional material indicates that future issues will include interviews with Latin American authors, information about periodicals, lists of reprints, and other features. The initial scope is hemispheric in that the list of publishers includes, besides the predictable preponderance from

---

* No. 2 of the *CBA* was also a quarterly issue. It became a bimonthly with No. 3, for July/August. With No. 4, September/October, received in March 1970, currency was approached. No. 3 carried a repetition of an earlier solicitation of data from publishers for an "anuario 1968" of books published in Spanish in Latin America. However, no mention of it was found in No. 4.

† At the suggestion and through the courtesy of Anne Gurvin, Director, Artigas-Washington Library, Montevideo, May 6, 1969.

Argentina, Uruguay, and Mexico, at least one each from Bolivia, Chile, Cuba, the Dominican Republic, Ecuador, Paraguay, Puerto Rico, and Venezuela. Incidentally, the term "American" is used, as it frequently is in the southern hemisphere, to refer exclusively to *Latin* America or, in this case, to Spanish America.

The most striking characteristic of the *CBA* is that it is colorful, both in terms of paper and ink and of the annotations provided for the books and periodicals listed. These are in English, usually descriptive but sometimes evaluative. The English is of the direct translation type, somewhat picturesque at times but usually intelligible. The phrase "English edition" is used on occasion, implying that there is also a Spanish one, but the editor states that none exists or is contemplated.* Scattered notes in Spanish are apparently directed primarily to publishers, who are urged to send their books in for listing. Prices are given for some items but are omitted for a surprising number. The extent to which the "CBA Editores" firm serves as a dealer is not clear. Several advertisements for Uruguayan bookstores are carried, but apparently the "annual edition" is to provide cumulated data and to offer at least some of the items for sale (pp. 42, 74, 78), at "special prices."

In terms of the state of the art it is difficult to appraise this new attempt at bibliographical coverage of current Spanish American publications. The editor of *Comentarios bibliográficos americanos* seemed sincere in his devotion to the cultural objective on an inter-American basis. Copies of the CBA are to be sent to Latin American publishers and dealers in exchange for data and publications. The subscription drive and sales markets are apparently aimed at the United States. This is realistic in that Latin American countries have made until now very little attempt to secure or to sell each others' works, a fact which indicates a lack of communication among them. On the other hand, representatives of institutions and firms from north of the border have been making their interest (often well financed) in securing Latin American materials increasingly evident.

In any case, the approach is novel, and the result makes fascinating reading. This "nonestablishment" attempt is somewhat hazy in outline at the beginning, but the editors invite constructive criticism. It may be that they have found a way—a self-supporting one—to circumvent in part the old nonfunctioning system of depending upon national libraries to carry out the time-consuming, expensive, and often thankless task of compiling national bibliography. The national libraries vary in their support, motivation, and effectiveness, but they are unfortunately usually underfunded

* Letter to this writer, dated August 21, 1969.

and understaffed. It would seem that this new commercial venture merits serious attention and whatever support can reasonably be given to it.

One ambitious attempt to compile a "Bibliografía de América Latina" must be reported upon here because of the importance of the project as background and also to correct published but inaccurate information concerning its existence. The UNESCO-sponsored *Bibliografía de Centroamérica y del Caribe* was published in 1958-1960, covering the years 1956-1959. It was basically a result of the efforts of Carlos Víctor Penna, Assistant Director for Cultural Affairs of the UNESCO Regional Center for the Western Hemisphere, but he was supported by a great deal of fine cooperative effort. In the 1950s UNESCO laid great emphasis on the creation of national commissions for bibliography. Where possible they would work in connection with the national library. In situations where those institutions were nonexistent or were ineffective in providing national bibliographies, it was hoped that industrious commission members would contribute their efforts, as a patriotic duty, to the assembling of information concerning publications currently produced in their countries. They would then either publish the information or supply it to some agency which might publish it.

The *Bibliografía de Centroamérica y del Caribe* covered the republics of the Antilles, Puerto Rico, and the six republics of Central America, including Panama. Data were assembled by the various national bibliographic commissions (or in such cases as Haiti and Puerto Rico, by the already recognized individual authorities on national bibliography) and were sent to Dr. Fermín Peraza in Havana. There, in the name of the Grupo Bibliográfico Nacional Cubano José Toribio Medina, they were edited and prepared for publication. Arrangement of the bibliography was by subject, without specific geographic approach. The project was funded for its first two years by an official Spanish agency, the Servicio de Publicaciones de la Junta Técnica de Archivos, Bibliotecas, y Museos de España, as a part of a centennial celebration. Peraza's introduction to the volume covering 1958 indicated that the work had proved so valuable that the subsidy was being extended for an additional two-year period. A preface by a Spanish official was dated January 1960. However, events in Cuba shortly thereafter completely altered the situation.

Bibliografía de Centroamérica y del Caribe, Argentina y Venezuela, the volume covering 1959, was published in 1961 in Havana. The preface, dated June 1960, acknowledged the financial support of the Comisión Cubana de la UNESCO. The Technical Director, Fermín Peraza, noted that for the first time, thanks to the modest funds secured from the sale of the

1956-1957 volumes, it had been possible to provide token remuneration to the *compiladores nacionales* who had contributed data for the bibliography. The volume covering 1960 was to have been sufficiently inclusive to be called "Bibliografía de América Latina." Announcement to this effect was made at an important and well-attended bibliographic conference held in Mexico in early December 1960. In anticipation of its appearance, the title change was made by one or more bibliographers. However, at that point Technical Director Fermín Peraza and his wife had fled Cuba, and following the conference they were to proceed to Colombia. Responsibility for the final compilation and editing of the "Bibliografía de América Latina" was accepted by the Instituto Bibliográfico Mexicano. There, so far as can be learned, the matter rests.

The episode of the *Bibliografía de Centroamérica y del Caribe* was important in various ways. It did demonstrate that under certain favorable circumstances, including volunteer labor and a publishing subsidy, it was possible to produce a well-organized and at least partial listing of the publications of several countries on a cooperative basis. As a classified bibliography, emphasis was on subject rather than country. Even so, in the *Bibliografía de Centroamérica y del Caribe,* the overall approach was regional. Whether the addition of Venezuela and, more particularly, Argentina was wise or represented overexpansion is an open question.

In any case, the experience illustrates difficulties inherent in such projects, for example: (1) the lack of effective laws of legal deposit made it difficult in some cases for individuals or groups to secure the essential information; (2) contributions were primarily dependent upon the professional and patriotic motivation of the national representatives; (3) a lack of bibliographic skills on the part of any contributor or his failure to comply with the formulae adopted resulted in heavy demands upon the technical director and any assistance available to him; (4) such a project required a financial subsidy for publication costs, even when the bibliography was compiled through services for which at best only token payment was to be expected; (5) there are possible hazards in attempting to expand an operating project farther and faster than financial and personnel resources may warrant.

II

SOUTH AMERICA

SOUTH AMERICA is a geographic entity as a continent, but despite the dreams and efforts of Simón Bolívar, continental identity otherwise is largely illusory. A variety of conferences have from time to time attempted to find or to build common interests in economic or social enterprise among the Spanish-speaking countries of the continent, but whatever results have been achieved have not carried over into bibliographic matters. It is indicative of the situation, for instance, that in practically any one of the best bookstores in the nine Spanish-speaking countries there would undoubtedly be more titles which were published in Spain than in all the South American republics combined.

South America is, therefore, not a significant division in bibliographical terms, but its use is traditional and at least serves to point up the great differences which exist among the Spanish-speaking countries. The case of Brazil is, of course, entirely apart. Under the circumstances, an alphabetical arrangement throughout seems in order.

ARGENTINA

For Argentina, in addition to sources previously listed as applicable to all countries, there are three fairly recent studies which provide useful back-

18

ground treatment of its bibliography. Two of these are by Josefa E. Sabor, the Director of the Centro de Investigaciones Bibliotecológicas. She contributed an article, "La bibliografía general argentina en curso de publicación," to the *Handbook of Latin American Studies* for 1963. In the second edition of her *Manual de fuentes de información,* published in Buenos Aires in 1967, Miss Sabor gives extensive consideration to the national bibliography of Argentina, although otherwise she provides only a brief general section on Latin America. Roberto Couture de Troismonts, the former Director de Bibliotecología de la Fundación Interamericana de Bibliotecología Franklin in Buenos Aires, contributed "The Present State of Argentine Current National Bibliography" as a working paper for the Tenth Seminar (Detroit, 1965).

Three titles described by these authorities must be accounted for: *Bibliografía argentina de artes y letras,* an important bibliography more general than the name would imply, published on a more or less quarterly basis by the Fondo Nacional de las Artes beginning in 1959; *Biblos: informativo bibliográfico*, published by the Cámara Argentina del Libro from 1941 until 1966, and the *Boletín bibliográfico nacional.* The *Boletín,* which originated in the late thirties, never became the important source of bibliography that the name would imply. It is in a comatose state if it has not actually expired. However, it, like the other two, merits individual description.

The *Bibliografía argentina de artes y letras* is at present the major source of information regarding Argentina's current national bibliography. The Fondo Nacional de las Artes assembles data from a variety of sources, including the Biblioteca de la Facultad de Filosofía y Letras de la Universidad de Buenos Aires. The scope of the bibliography is broadly interpreted, so that selective coverage is provided for most nonscientific or technical materials. Bibliographic techniques are excellent. Data are arranged by the Universal Decimal System, and an index is provided. Number 20, October/December 1965, provided a cumulative index to that date. In addition to the *BAAL* itself, special bibliographies, called *compilaciones especiales*, have been published as supplements, beginning in 1962 with number 13.

The bibliography was subsidized originally to the extent that it could be distributed gratis or on exchange. However, recipients were informed in December 1968 that beginning with number 35/36 for July/December 1967, it was available only by subscription through the Editorial Sudamericano. It is hoped that adequate support will be provided to enable this useful and well-presented bibliography to continue to function.

Biblos, after appearing more or less regularly for a quarter of a century as the organ of the Cámara Argentina del Libro, ceased publication in 1966. The Director of the Cámara, Sr. Adolfo Jasco, stated to this writer* that he considered the bulletin no longer essential, since *Fichero* can now provide the same type of information and can do so in more organized form. Sr. Jasco indicated also that financial reasons were a consideration in the demise of *Biblos.* He said that book production in Argentina had declined considerably within the past two years or so. (Presumably, political as well as economic factors would account for the great decrease, since a significant portion of Argentina's substantial writing is done by university professors, many of whom have recently absented themselves from the country.)

The *Boletín bibliográfico nacional* should theoretically be the official source for the national bibliography, but its history and present status illustrate the full range of difficulties to which such publications are subject. It was originated by a nonprofessional group, a Comisión Nacional de Cultura, and it experienced a succession of sponsors before it was finally handed over to the Biblioteca Nacional several years ago. The Biblioteca, which suffers for one thing from an ineffective *ley de depósito legal,* does not have at hand the current materials to provide the information needed, nor has it been provided with qualified staff to carry out the assignment. The chief virtue of the *Boletín* is that it does provide some sort of a continuous record from 1937 through 1956. Number 34 (1957/58) has long been reported "in preparation." The circumstances would seem to justify Josefa Sabor's severe criticism and her opinion that it would be well to close out the *Boletín* and provide a successor which merits the title it bears.

In his above-mentioned paper for the Tenth Seminar (1965) Roberto Couture de Troismonts, after analyzing the unsatisfactory situation as of that date, stated that the Fundación Interamericana de Bibliotecología Franklin, located in Buenos Aires, had drawn up a cooperative plan which would provide full coverage. A commission representing the various groups concerned had met in October and November 1964, and had agreed upon a project.

Several publications were to be established: (1) a "Boletín bibliográfico semanal" would provide a basic record of works listed in the Registro Nacional de la Propiedad Intelectual. *Biblos,* to be continued by the Cámara Argentina del Libro along its former lines, would provide a monthly record, complementary to that of the proposed "Boletín,"

* Interview, May 2, 1969.

including advertising and titles which had not been registered. The *Bibliografía argentina de artes y letras* would continue to be published quarterly by the Fondo Nacional de las Artes, with its present characteristics. A "Bibliografía científica argentina," projected by the Consejo Nacional de Investigaciones Científicas y Técnicas, would provide a quarterly record of scientific publications, including an analytic catalog of articles of some 200 journals. Partly because a considerable number of university publications were involved, it was thought that the Instituto Bibliotecológico de la Universidad de Buenos Aires would be able to undertake this compilation. The same Instituto would compile data about university publications throughout the country. The Biblioteca Nacional, having been provided with information by so many sources, would publish the *Boletín bibliográfico nacional* on either a semester or an annual basis.

This complicated scheme, with its varied participants working on a voluntary and cooperative basis, did not get off the ground. However, the proposal did point up the need, and it did stimulate thought as to other possible means of attaining the desired objectives.

Four years after Couture de Troismonts presented his paper on "The Present State of Argentine Current National Bibliography" and a plan for its improvement to the Tenth Seminar, a paper prepared for the Fourteenth Seminar (1969) provided an updated report on the situation and a new proposal. "El panorama bibliográfico documental en la Argentina," by Hans Gravenhorst, Director of the Bibliographical Institute of the University of Buenos Aires, reported succinctly on the current bibliographical situation, on a substitute plan, and on a new proposal for handling official publications.

Mr. Gravenhorst stated that the bibliographic panorama had not changed substantially in the past four years. The nearest approach to a general bibliography was still the *Bibliografía argentina de artes y letras*. This continued to be supplemented (and to some extent duplicated) by specialized bibliographies published by the Instituto Bibliográfico de la Plata: *Bibliografía argentina de ciencias de la educación, Bibliografía argentina de filosofía,* and *Bibliografía argentina de psicología.* The Centro Documental de la Estación Experimental Agropecuaria de Pergamino was about to publish an 18-volume compilation of agricultural bibliography, "Bibliografía agrícola argentina de 1795-1964," which it planned to keep up to date by means of supplementary volumes.

Mr. Gravenhorst reported also that the second edition of the *Catálogo colectivo de publicaciones periódicas existentes en bibliotecas científicas y técnicas argentinas,* compiled by the Asociación de Bibliotecas Científicas y Técnicas under the direction of Ernesto Gietz and published in 1962 by the Consejo Nacional de Investigaciones Científicas y Técnicas, was being updated. The third edition was expected to contain some 20,000 titles. Useful as such a union list would be, it is of course too general to be considered as national bibliography.

The plan for the cooperative compiling of the national bibliography, as outlined by Roberto Couture de Troismonts in his 1965 paper, had involved too many different entities to prove practicable. However, the University of Buenos Aires was working on a plan which it was hoped might successfully coordinate the efforts of a more homogeneous group. The University maintains the most extensive bibliographic records in the country in the form of its union catalog, compiled by its Bibliographical Institute. The Institute was studying a proposal made by the Junta de Bibliotecas Nacionales Universitarias Argentinas in a meeting held in Tucumán in May 1969. It called initially for the combining of the catalogs of the other eleven national universities in Argentina with that of the UBA. The next step would be to incorporate the holdings of important non-university libraries, thus forming a great centralized catalog of national scope.

Mr. Gravenhorst had previously commented to this writer* that the UBA already acquires some 70 percent of Argentine publications, and he believed it could secure the remainder or at least obtain data concerning it. The provincial universities would presumably cooperate to provide information about regional and specialized situations. Other nonuniversity libraries would be encouraged to cooperate. The Cámara Argentina del Libro (which is a commercial concern formed to provide services to publishers) would probably cooperate as far as possible. Eventually, the Registro Nacional de la Propiedad Intelectual and others would be encouraged to cooperate.

Assuming that the UBA has at its disposal a sufficiently large body of bibliographic data to provide a viable basis for a national bibliography, the question arises as to how the data could be processed to be made available in published form. Here, also, Argentina has a proposed solution to the problem. In his SALALM paper, Mr. Gravenhorst makes a one-sentence statement covering what seems a revolutionary proposal in terms of national bibliography of the South American continent: "The Consejo [Nacional de Investigaciones Científicas y Técnicas] plans to process the information by computers and to prepare an offset publication from the

* Interview in Buenos Aires, May 2, 1969.

printout, an undertaking which it hopes to carry out by the end of next year."

That this hope appears well founded was confirmed by an interview* with Mr. Gravenhorst and his colleague Dr. Juan A. García-Roméu, Director Ejecutivo, Centro de Investigaciones y Aplicación de la Informática, Universidad Nacional de Buenos Aires. Dr. García-Roméu, who had worked with Mr. Gravenhorst in formulating the plan, is a recognized authority in his field and is enthusiastic about the possibilities of helping to provide Argentina with its much needed national bibliography. At the time the chief problem appeared to be a financial one.

The extent to which official government publications were included in Mr. Gravenhorst's estimate that 70 percent of the national bibliographic output was held by the university system was not stated. However, official publications are, in general, among the types least well represented in Latin American national libraries, since they are not covered by copyright and there seems scant effort to bring them under such *leyes de depósito* as do exist.

Mr. Gravenhorst concluded his SALALM paper with a recommendation for the establishment in every Latin American country of a centralized agency charged with the assembling of all official publications issued by that country. His eleven-point proposal included recommendations that the centralized collecting agency should disperse the publications to suitable recipients, but before doing so should note them and should publish at least semiannually a bulletin listing them. The agency might be a part of a country's existing documentation center, if any, a part of the national university or national library, or it might be established as a separate entity.

Fichero bibliográfico hispanoamericano, published by Bowker Editores Argentina, assembles and organizes a great deal of information about the trade books published in Argentina and at least representative titles from institutes and university presses. Since Argentina and Mexico are the two leaders in book production of the Spanish American countries, it is natural that they should be the most extensively represented in *Fichero.* A count of the firms listed as contributing to three consecutive issues in 1969 (March-May) showed that, as compared with Mexico and Spain, also a heavy contributor, Argentina ranked in the three months second, first, and third respectively, with an average of 26 percent. Of course the actual number of entries would vary with the catalogs analyzed. In any case, no geographical approach is provided.

* May 2, 1969.

Catalogs of Argentine publishers and book dealers vary greatly in extent, organization, and data provided. Probably the most extensive is *Libros de Argentina: Catálogo bibliográfico de la distribuidora Tres Américas*. Its 240-page volume, dated February 1969, claims to be the export-import representative of more than 150 Argentine publishing houses. The firms are listed alphabetically. A subject index of sorts is provided, but there is none for authors. Several publishers and bookstores publish sales lists which they call "bibliographic bulletins." They provide varying amounts of data concerning their limited offerings. None seems extensive or important enough to be considered a significant factor in national bibliography.

Summary

The most important current source of Argentine national bibliography is the *Bibliografía argentina de artes y letras*, which is more general than the title indicates, but whose status is somewhat uncertain for financial reasons. Of earlier publications, *Biblos* has ceased publication and has been partially superseded by *Fichero*. The *Boletín bibliográfico argentino*, never robust and handed to the Biblioteca Nacional in an enfeebled condition several years ago, seems about to expire in the care of an organization unequipped to infuse new life into what should theoretically be the vehicle for the publication of the current national bibliography.

On the other hand, Argentina has an alive book world which has begun to consider alternative courses. It has a university system with resources in current and continuing bibliographical records, in equipment, and in expertise which present the possibility of bypassing a situation where the law of legal deposit does not function and the National Library is un-equipped to provide leadership in bibliographical matters. The outcome may be the first computerized national bibliography in the Americas. The head of the Bibliographic Center of the University of Buenos Aires, in a paper presented to the Fourteenth Seminar (1969), made a brief statement concerning present plans and hopes, and he advanced a proposal for the establishing of collecting agencies and bibliographic control of official government publications. These possibilities, if realized, would break new ground and could revolutionize bibliographical procedures in Latin America.

Little has been said, apparently, about Argentine periodicals, but a great many of them are in fact official publications and so would be included in any comprehensive records of those.

BOLIVIA

Bolivia is a country which suffers from some of the worst ailments known to afflict the book trade in any country, and it adds some unique ones of its own. Like other countries of the Andean area, it has a population which is preponderantly illiterate, and many of its people do not speak or read Spanish. It has a great range of altitude and difficult communication problems. It has no paper mills and must import all paper stock used.

Other countries have transportation problems, but Bolivia's range is from the highest capital city in the hemisphere to the near sea level of the Amazon basin. Only Bolivia has neither a sea coast nor an outlet through a navigable river, but it is not the only country which has to import paper and as an economy measure to print its publications on paper of such poor quality that its deterioration rate makes them a high risk investment in terms of durability. One strikingly unique problem is that two cities lay claim to being the capital city. Sucre seems definitely to have lost the contest to La Paz as the seat of government, but it contains the National Library to which national publications are, theoretically, required to be sent on deposit.

When Peter de la Garza wrote a special article for the *Handbook of Latin American Studies* (1961), "Records of Current Publication in Bolivia, Ecuador, and Honduras," a common denominator of the three countries was their lack of "anything remotely resembling a national bibliography." He stated that in early 1960 the Asociación Boliviana de Bibliotecarios succeeded in getting through Congress a bill establishing a national bibliographic commission which would be responsible for the compilation of the national bibliography. Whether the President had signed it, and if so, whether there had been any efforts to implement it, he did not know. The few possibilities he could suggest as sources of information included periodicals of doubtful continuity, two mimeographed book lists of which one was dated 1956, and the first two of the Stechert-Hafner special catalogs listing publications acquired under the Latin American Cooperative Acquisitions Project.

However, the Bolivian situation shows what can be done by individuals who have the knowledge, energy, and resources to deal with even so difficult a situation. The two individuals chiefly concerned are the authors of an informative, five-part paper on "Book Publishing in Bolivia," contributed to the Ninth Seminar (1964). The two are Marcela Meneses, a librarian, and Werner Guttentag, Managing Director of the Editorial Los Amigos del Libro, based in Cochabamba. The most relevant sections of the paper for present purposes are the first two: "Present Status of the Publishing Industry" and "Bibliography."

The authors were able to state that "a systematic bibliographical work" for 1962 had been published by Los Amigos del Libro publishers and that the 1963 volume would be available in the near future. It is a pleasure to report that annual volumes of *Bibliografía boliviana* have continued to appear under the name of Werner Guttentag as author, and that they are available in hardback as well as in paper cover. The volume covering 1967 bears a colophon date of September 6, 1968. It contains, as have previous volumes, supplements for the individual years since 1962. The arrangement continues to be alphabetical by author, with classification indicated by a Dewey decimal number. A title index is provided. A new feature, which it is proposed to extend, is the annotation of some items.

Much of the information contained in *Bibliografía boliviana* is made available earlier by means of catalogs distributed by the publisher. In his *Handbook* article Garza noted an early carbon-copy version of the catalog of the Librería Los Amigos del Libro. Apparently it became soon thereafter a printed, numbered, and dated list, first as *Libros nacionales*, later as *Libros bolivianos*. An 8-page newsprint catalog, it listed both current and out-of-print titles. The publisher was indicated only for the firm's own titles, and the price was omitted for a surprisingly large number of items. These lists were discontinued, apparently, with number 62, for November/December 1967. A *Catálogo 1968* of the Editorial Los Amigos del Libro bearing a colophon date of August 28, 1968, seems to have superseded the bimonthly lists. The 55-page catalog of the firm's publications is apparently meant to be accompanied by a price list, presumably subject to change without notice, as were those of the bulletin. Books are presented in large groupings, with scant attention to the alphabet. However, the catalog is valuable for its rather detailed descriptions of the books listed, information which in many cases is not otherwise available.

Los Amigos del Libro is the firm listed by *Fichero bibliográfico hispanoamericano* and *Comentarios bibliográficos americanos* as the source of their information concerning Bolivian publications.*

Until the Librería Los Amigos del Libro came on the scene, we were

---

* The existence of a *Boletín bibliográfico boliviano*, edited by Antonio Paredes Candia, has been called to my attention by Carl Deal. The first issue, Año 1, no. 1, was dated junio 1965. He states that it has been continued at least through Año 1, no. 6, mayo 1968 (all issues, 1965-1968, being numbered "Año 1"). From the title page of the first issue, a copy of which was provided, the bulletin appears to be like numerous other "bibliographic bulletins." A few current titles were listed, but, to judge by the table of contents, the bulletin was devoted primarily to book-related news.

dependent almost entirely upon catalogs from bookdealers elsewhere for information about Bolivian publications—an indirect and unsatisfactory source of bibliography. It is still true that booklists of some of the better foreign dealers supply useful supplementary data. For instance, E. Iturriaga of Lima provides semiannual lists of some twenty-five Bolivian titles by various publishers, with full bibliographical data. García Cambeiro of Buenos Aires and other dealers occasionally provide special catalogs or lists of Bolivian books.

As of late 1969 a new development is under way which could have significant bearing upon the state of the art of Bolivian bibliography. In November and December several extensive lists were sent out by Montalvo Book Dealers, which offered current and retrospective publications with full data. The enterprise is headed by Alfredo F. Montalvo, a Bolivian with a library science degree from a North American university who recently served in an interim capacity on the staff of the University of Florida Libraries. A December list from him included an experimental listing of "forthcoming" books.* Mr. Montalvo is interested also in the possibilities of providing government documents and is conferring on the matter with Mrs. Rosa Q. Mesa, Chairman of the SALALM Committee on Latin American Government Documents.

A major work on the retrospective bibliography of Bolivia, which has only recently appeared, deserves notice for itself and for its possible influence upon the development of current bibliographical records. A massive *Catálogo de la bibliografía boliviana: libros y folletos 1900-1963*, by Arturo Costa de la Torre, was published in La Paz under the sponsorship of the Universidad Mayor de San Andrés. It bears a title page date of 1966, but a colophon date attests the printer's having finished his work on the last day of 1968. The period covered extends from the last major work of the noted Bolivian bibliographer, Gabriel René Moreno (1836-1908), down to 1963. Reference is made in preliminary "Advertencias generales" to a supplement as being "in press," but that appears to be a matter of addenda to the original volume rather than a continuation. However, in the introduction the author speaks strongly of the need for developments in library and bibliographic organization which would make possible the development of an *anuario bibliográfico*.

The *Catálogo* is important not only for its great contribution to

* A letter from Mr. Montalvo dated March 18, 1970, indicates, with regard to "forthcoming books," that he has found the term "in press," as used by Bolivian publishers, to be a very relative matter. However, he is continuing his attempt to secure definite advance information, and he thinks he has made some progress.

twentieth-century bibliography but for two other reasons—the lengthy introduction and the biographical information provided. The author states that of the numerous questionnaires sent out, over seven hundred replies were received. The information thus provided makes the *Catálogo* an important source of near-current Bolivian national biography as well as of bibliography.

Of himself, Costa de la Torre says that he is an "historian, biographer, genealogist, and bibliographer." His other published works are primarily of an historical nature. He stated in the introduction that he had spent three arduous years in the preparation of the *Catálogo*—an easily believable statement. It is to be hoped that he may be instrumental in helping Bolivia to develop a really comprehensive current national bibliography.*

Summary

The Bolivian situation presents some unique difficulties, but it also illustrates what competent and energetic individuals can do. Bolivia had lacked until recently any consistent record of its national bibliography during the twentieth century. However, since 1962 annual volumes of *Bibliografía boliviana*, compiled by Werner Guttentag, have appeared regularly and promptly. Los Amigos del Libro, a publishing firm and bookstore with which Guttentag is connected, provides data to *Fichero bibliográfico hispanoamericano* and to *Comentarios bibliográficos americanos*. For additional information concerning current publications of other firms, we have been dependent chiefly upon that provided by occasional bookdealers' lists from elsewhere. At present, however, a young Bolivian with a graduate degree in library science is actively engaged in the book trade. Beginning with the fall of 1969, Alfredo F. Montalvo has provided useful lists of Bolivian publications, including current titles. He has attempted to supply also information about "forthcoming books." His activities, although presumably temporary, may produce some lasting results.

A recently published *Catálogo de la bibliografía boliviana: libros y folletos, 1900-1963,* by Arturo Costa de la Torre, provides the most extensive record of Bolivian publishing since the later years of Gabriel René Moreno (1836-1908), Bolivia's most noted bibliographer. Although the *Catálogo* must now be considered retrospective, it includes biographical information about most of Bolivia's contemporary writers. The author

---

* Alfredo Montalvo, in the above cited letter, says that Sr. Costa de la Torre is working as time permits on a major historical work, but that at present his political activities are leaving him scant time to devote to either history or bibliography.

indicates full understanding of the importance of a current national bibliography for Bolivia. It is possible that he may be instrumental in helping to achieve this end.

BRAZIL

Brazil, the Portuguese-speaking country which occupies half the South American continent, is a case apart. No Latin American country has been more ready to learn from others and to adapt new bibliographic techniques to its own uses, so far as circumstances permit, than has Brazil. Brazil's library development began in the 1930s, at which time the Dewey Decimal System was introduced by a North American librarian through a course offered at McKenzie College in São Paulo. The country remains a strong champion of the decimal system, though now primarily of the Universal rather than the Dewey version.

Since the formation of UNESCO and its epoch-making Conference on the Improvement of Bibliographical Services in November 1950, Brazilian librarians have worked closely with that body. In 1954 UNESCO was instrumental in establishing the Instituto Brasileiro de Bibliografia y Documentação, the IBBD, which became and is a potent constructive force. The international aspects of the work of the IBBD were described by Abner L. Corrêa Vicentini in an article in the January 1969 issue of *Library Trends,* "The Organization of National Documentation and Information Services in Latin America, with Special Reference to Brazil."

On the domestic scene Brazil has prodigious problems to deal with in attempting to acquire and to record the publications issued throughout the country. Some of the reasons why Brazil has problems of the magnitude it does were enumerated by Peter de la Garza in a paper, "The Acquisition of Research Materials from Brazil and Their Selection," prepared for the Eighth Seminar (1963). He said in part:

> Many economic and social features, over which even an aggressive librarian has no control, contribute to the unfortunate situation. Among them may be cited the improvisatory nature of enterprise in a rapidly developing country; an expanding but chronically disturbed economy; a complex federal government structure which on several occasions has verged on chaos; a highly competitive book trade forced by inflationary pressures to reduce overhead costs and minimize long term operations; and lack of coordination between governmental and private agencies concerned with bibliographic endeavors.

Since 1963 political problems have worsened, and press censorship is an ever present reality. The phrase "Brazilian-type inflation" has become synonymous with "runaway" inflation. The book trade suffers doubly under these conditions, and so do related activities.

Under the circumstances it is a credit to Brazil that its bibliographers and publishers have been able to do as much as they have to provide records of its national book production. The problems inherent in the size and diversity of the country, including the recognized fact that it lacks an effective postal system, seem for the present insoluble. In some cases regional agencies, notably universities, are attempting to assemble collections of local materials with their corresponding bibliographical records. These will some day be useful in assembling a retrospective national bibliography, but their present contribution to current bibliography is limited.*

There are at present three principal sources of more or less current national bibliography. Of these, the longest lived and the one which is presumably the official record is the *Boletim bibliográfico* (1886-), published by the Biblioteca Nacional in Rio de Janeiro at intervals from 1886. The current series began in 1951. It is, with its limitations, one of the best national bibliographies published in Latin America. It is arranged on a classified system (Dewey), but its excellent index provides approaches by author and subject. Documents are included. A particularly valuable feature is the inclusion in the second semestral volume of as comprehensive a list of periodicals currently published throughout the country as it can assemble, with official publications starred. The basic arrangement is classified, but there is a title index.

The limitations are those imposed by conditions over which the Biblioteca Nacional has no control. The law of legal deposit is poorly observed in the country as a whole, and as is true elsewhere, official agencies are prone to forget that their publications are of interest to others than the unit immediately served. Since the preparation of the *Boletim* is done by the Acquisitions Department of the Library on the basis of materials actually received, the record, while technically superior, is incomplete. Financial problems are reflected in the lengthening gap between the dates of the material covered and date of publication, e.g., the second volume for 1964 was distributed late in 1968.

Bibliografia brasileira (1938/39-), another official Brazilian bibliography, is currently the more up to date of the two. It is prepared and published by the Instituto Nacional do Livro, an agency of the Ministerio

---

* This aspect of the situation is touched upon by Vicentini (1969), p. 255.

de Educação e Cultura. The present editorial committee is headed by Aureo Ottoni (under whose name entries occur in the *Handbook of Latin American Studies*). The retrospective volumes covering the years 1938/39 through 1955 were published at irregular intervals from 1941 to 1957.

From 1956 through early 1962 the Instituto do Livro made its bibliographic records available through its quarterly review, the *Revista do livro* (1956-). "Bibliografia brasileira corrente" was presented as a colored-page section, subject to removal if desired. It was the expressed intention that the data would later be cumulated in additional volumes of *Bibliografia brasileira*. The *Revista do livro* suspended publication in 1961 (ano 6, no. 23/24). It resumed in March 1964 (ano 6, no. 25) and completed publication of the 1961 bibliography. A second issue was published in 1964, with a bibliographic section for early 1962, after which there was another interval. The section "Bibliografia brasileira corrente" has not been published since 1964.

Issues for 1965 and 1966 were later published as double numbers (27/28 and 29/30) in order to update the review. A prefatory note in each stated that the bibliography for the years that would normally have been represented (1963 and 1964 respectively) had been omitted so as not to delay further the updating of the *Revista*, but that the data would appear in later volumes of *Bibliografia brasileira*. Early in 1967 (no. 31) the *Revista* resumed its publication as a quarterly review—an excellent one, with valuable special bibliographies but without the earlier section on current national bibliography.

In 1966 another volume of *Bibliografia brasileira* appeared, this time one for 1963, leaving uncumulated for the present the period covered by the *Revista do livro*, 1955-1962. The Instituto has been making progress towards current publications of the later annual volumes. Those for 1964, 1965, and 1966 had been published by 1967. The 1967 volume was scheduled to appear in the spring of 1968, thus bringing publication of the annual volumes up to date. It may well have done so, but information to that effect is not at hand.*

Bibliografia brasileira mensal entered the picture in November 1967. (The issues of the first volume were numbered through 14 in order to begin volume 2, 1968, on a calendar year basis.) It is, as the title would

---

* A letter from Jerry R. James, Field Director, Library of Congress Office, Brazil, dated April 7, 1970, states that there was a plan for the Instituto to publish a cumulated bibliography for the years 1962-1967, but it has been abandoned. The 1967 volume may be issued separately if there are funds to do so. Mr. James is to present a paper on the work of the Library of Congress Office and related topics to the Fifteenth Seminar, to be held in Toronto, Canada, June 23-26, 1970.

indicate, the monthly edition of Brazilian national bibliography, as prepared and published by the Instituto do Livro. It thus supersedes the "Bibliografia brasileira corrente" formerly published in the quarterly issues of *Revista do livro*. The editor is Aureo Ottoni, who has also edited the recent annual volumes. *Bibliografia brasileira mensal* is, like the annual volumes, arranged by the Dewey Decimal System. Entries are complete, including price. The data cover all fields and are current, so the monthly editions are useful acquisition tools. They do, however, lack an author index.

One of the reasons for the prompt and relatively complete coverage by the *Bibliografia brasileira mensal* is the existence of a cooperative arrangement between the Instituto do Livro and the Library of Congress. This arrangement was set up in Rio de Janeiro in or about 1967 to provide LC with selective, but much more extensive, coverage of Brazilian publications than had been possible previously. Books are catalogued at the Rio office.* A desk is provided for a representative of the Instituto to avail himself of whatever information he may need. A systematic effort is made to secure materials from various other parts of Brazil.

BBB: Boletim bibliográfico brasileiro: revista dos editôres, which was published from 1952 to 1967 by Estante Publicações, was a commercial enterprise, sponsored by various agencies interested in the production and sale of books. It was during most of that time the most nearly current source of information concerning Brazilian publications. It was arranged by the Dewey Decimal System, but each issue had an author index, thereby greatly enhancing its bibliographical value. It served its commercial purpose well for a time, but it became a victim of Brazilian economic difficulties.

Edições brasileiras: catálago trimestral de livros publicados no Brasil, published in Rio de Janeiro from 1963 to 1966 by the Sindicato Nacional

---

* This practice may have been suspended as an economy move by the U.S. government. A bulletin published by the Library of Congress on August 4, 1969, dealing with the status of funding for fiscal 1970 under Title II of the Higher Education Act of 1965 as amended, reported on reductions in the National Program for Acquisitions and Cataloging. The relevant Paragraph 3 follows: "The shared cataloging program for Brazilian publications has had to be terminated and the NPAC office in Rio de Janeiro has reverted to its original function as an acquisitions office for Brazilian publications. Publications will continue to receive LACAP numbers assigned in Brazil and all LACAP selections will continue to receive high priority cataloging at LC. . . ." (*NPAC Progress Report* No. 9, August 4, 1969, p. 2.) Fortunately, the *Bibliografia brasileira mensal* has so far survived difficulties in both countries. The November/ December issue, received by the Hispanic Foundation at the Library of Congress by March 1970, not only appeared promptly but contained a full author and title index for 1969. (Telephone conversation with Donald F. Wisdom, March 25, 1970.)

dos Editôres de Livros, was also a commercial enterprise but was never successful as such. The three issues, especially the first, contained extensive and complete bibliographical data about the offerings of various publishers, with author and title indexes. The experiment was more successful as bibliography than as a means of selling books. In 1968 a 153-page volume, *Bibliografia brasileira de livros infantis,* compiled by the Centro de Bibliotécnica, was published by the Sindicato Nacional dos Editôres de Livros as a special supplement to *Edições brasileiras,* but the Executive Secretary of the Syndicate, Hélio Araújo, indicated to this writer that there was no intention of resuming publication of *Edições.*

There was, however, another project for the preparation and production of national bibliography on a cooperative basis of which Mr. Araújo spoke very hopefully in April 1969,* as did also a representative of the Instituto Brasileiro de Bibliografia e Documentação† (IBBD). The agencies which were parties to the cooperative project were, besides those named, the Biblioteca Nacional and the Ministry of Education. The basic document was the *Ata de Primera Reunião dos Orgãos Encarregados do Levantamento da Bibliografia Nacional, Realizado em 25.07.1968.* It was discussed and accepted on July 25, 1968, as a working agreement subject to the necessary official approval.

The basic essential, the collection of the publications to be recorded, would be met by a division of labor: (1) commercial publications would be secured by the Sindicato dos Editôres, which would guarantee the acquisition of 90 percent of such materials; (2) official publications would be collected by (a) IBBD, (b) the Biblioteca Nacional, and (c) the Ministry of Education, with the latter responsible for securing from the universities their theses and reports. Once the materials were acquired, they would be catalogued by two agencies—the IBBD which would do the specialized works, and the Biblioteca Nacional which would do the general ones. The data would then be utilized to prepare a truly comprehensive and up-to-date national bibliography. It would appear monthly with quarterly cumulations and, when possible, annual ones.

Mr. Araújo stated that the groups had reacted favorably to the proposal and that the necessary intergroup arrangements could be made soon, after which the proposal would go to the Presidency of the Republic for the necessary decree law to be issued. He considered the prospects for approval to be excellent and thought it probable that the program could

---

* Interview, April 22, 1969.
† Interview, April 24, 1969.

be gotten under way by 1970. A letter dated August 20, 1969, stated that the decree had not yet been forthcoming, but efforts were being made to secure it, and information would be provided as to progress when and if they were successful in securing the authorization. However, President Arturo Costa e Silva was incapacitated by a stroke on August 31, and a military junta assumed power. No further word concerning the cooperative project has been received since that time.

The Instituto Brasileiro de Bibliografia e Documentação, which was mentioned earlier, is an agency to which full justice cannot be done here, since its bibliographic work is primarily in scientific fields rather than in national bibliography as such. However, of its specialized bibliographies two are of such a nature that they should be included. The *Bibliografia brasileira de ciências sociais* (1954-), an annual volume, appears considerably behind its date but is still published. In 1968 a new edition of *Periódicos brasileiros de cultura* updated the "provisional one" of 1956. The new edition lists 2,049 periodicals currently published in Brazil, chiefly in the fields of the humanities and the social sciences, and with as full bibliographical data as were available. It is planned to issue supplements as needed.*

Two SALALM working papers have dealt with Brazilian bibliography. "The Situation of Bibliography in Brazil," contributed by Irene Doria for the Ninth Seminar (1964), provides excellent background and a descriptive account of the national bibliography as of that date. She considered its state to be unsatisfactory, but found more cause for satisfaction in specialized bibliographies, to which a considerable portion of the paper was devoted. Of those listed several are still continuing, and two of the more important ones have not yet been mentioned. The Centro Brasileiro de Pesquisas Educacionais publishes a quarterly bulletin, *Bibliografia brasileira de educação,* which indexes selected material from books, periodicals, and newspapers. It was and continues to be the source of data provided to the *Handbook of Latin American Studies* for its biennial sections on education. The highly important Centro Latino-Americano de Pesquisas em Ciências Sociais, which originated under UNESCO auspices in 1957, publishes a valuable bimonthly bulletin, *Bibliografia* (1962-). It lists books received by the Center's library and indexes articles in the periodicals received. The bibliography, which is sent free to subscribers to the Center's quarterly review *América Latina,* may also be subscribed to independently for a nominal price. It is undoubtedly the most important

* For a fuller description, see the *LC Information Bulletin* 27:42 (Oct. 17, 1968), p. 634.

index of the kind in Latin America, and it is unfortunate that for financial reasons it appears in mimeographed form on poor quality paper.

The Doria paper concluded with a three-part appendix listing 182 bibliographies. Miss Doria stated that she had tried to indicate in the body of her paper all the bibliographies listed from 1950 to 1964. Both the text of her paper and the appended bibliography of bibliographies are of continuing value.

In 1966 Maria Antonia Ferraz, a professor in the São Paulo Library School, provided the Eleventh Seminar with a bibliography of reference works on Brazil. The nine-page list, arranged by the decimal system classification, contains some 175 items. It provides useful information, but there is no text, nor is there an author index.

Summary

The last paragraph of the Doria paper seems to summarize so well the progressive attitudes of the top Brazilian bibliographies that it may well be quoted here: "We hope to have indicated that, even if the work done so far is not perfect, we know that bibliographic work is of great value, and we know what can and should be done. This is a guarantee of future progress and improvement."

Brazil is fortunate in that publishers, bookdealers, and bibliographers recognize their common interests. Whether or not conditions will soon permit trying out their cooperative plan, which has been drawn up, the fact of its creation is in itself significant. Meanwhile, although subject to limitation in coverage, the current national bibliography of Brazil is excellent in many respects and seems headed upward.

CHILE

Of the South American countries Chile is the one with the strongest bibliographical tradition, thanks to a number of notable bibliographers, among whom the most outstanding was of course José Toribio Medina. However, after Medina's death in 1930, there was a long interval when the principal records were lists contained in periodicals, miscellaneous specialized bibliographies, and a publisher's catalog. In 1961 the Zimmerman *Guide to Current Latin American Periodicals* listed only the *Anuario de publicaciones periódicas chilenas* as a continuing official source of data concerning national periodicals, but one which had been in abeyance from

1938 until 1951. The volume covering 1958 was received in 1961. Otherwise, the journal *Atenea* was considered the most important source, followed by the quarterly list, *Servicio bibliográfico chileno.*

The paper on "Current Bibliography in Chile" contributed by Blanca Matas to the Eighth Seminar (1963) provided only a brief background statement and listings of (1) bibliographies published since 1930, (2) journals in which partial bibliographies might be found, and (3) publishers whose catalogs might prove useful.

In view of the importance attached to records provided by periodicals, it seems in order to report, regretfully, that several of the major ones have suspended or ceased publication. An item in a Chilean newspaper, *El Mercurio,* for May 11, 1969, stated that the crises in Chilean universities had caused *Finis Terrae* to cease publication and had interrupted the publication of *Atenea* and of the *Anales de la Universidad de Chile* (founded in 1843). This leaves *Mapocho,* organ of the Biblioteca Nacional, as the only outstanding cultural and literary review currently published. In terms of bibliography, one of its regular features was until recently a cumulated listing of the publications of the BN, a feature which it is to be hoped will soon be resumed.

Carl Deal, in his paper for the Twelfth Seminar (1967), "Bibliographic Aids for Collecting Current Latin American Materials," listed two items, both of which continue to serve their different objectives. *Servicio bibliográfico chileno* is a quarterly bookdealer's list which is unique in several ways. The *Anuario de la prensa chilena* was first published by the Biblioteca Nacional in 1887, covering the years 1877 to 1885. It suspended publication in 1916 but resumed in 1962, soon after Don Guillermo Feliú Cruz (1901-), secretary to and disciple of José Toribio Medina (1852-1930), was placed in charge of the Dirección General de Bibliotecas, Archivos, y Museos. In the interval since the death of Medina in 1930, there had been published only the volume for 1877-1885, under the direction of Raúl Silva Castro, and the partial record irregularly supplied by the *Anuario de publicaciones periódicas.*

The *Anuario* is an exhaustive record of the country's bibliographic production, in so far as that production reaches the BN. The *ley de depósito* has fortunately been observed rather well in Chile, so that most publications of importance are included. Valuable as it is, it provides no subject approach to materials listed. The present Director of the Biblioteca Nacional, Sr. Roque Esteban Scarpa, indicates that the institution would be very happy to provide fuller records concerning the national bibliography if funds were available. It has done some retrospective indexing of older literary periodicals, and is currently producing a bibliography of critical reviews of Chilean literary works.

Meanwhile, in addition to the valuable but traditional services being rendered by the BN, other agencies are developing important programs. New forces are constructively at work, and results should be increasingly evident. A major stimulus is provided by the fact that Santiago is the seat of the United Nations' Economic Commission for Latin America (ECLA), or in Spanish, the Comisión Económica para la América Latina–CEPAL, as it is commonly known.

Another healthy development in Chile is a growing realization on the part of its Congress that knowledge of the past is an essential factor in making wise daily decisions affecting the present and future. A Comisión de Restauración de la Biblioteca del Congreso, established as a joint commission in 1968, is supporting a major program for the indexing of Chilean newspapers. Lautaro Valenzuela, Ximena Cruz (daughter of Don Guillermo Feliú Cruz), and Edmundo Seraní constitute the capable team in charge. The program calls for current indexing of all the newspapers of the country, including those of the provinces. The aim is to cover on a selective basis all matters of national or international concern. The index is being done on a subject and name basis, dating from 1963. The Restoration Commission is interested in retrospective indexing as well. Files include cards covering the years 1942-1963, selected on the basis of earlier criteria, and there are some cards analyzing newspapers back to the nineteenth century. This file, called a "Catálogo de la prensa chilena," is open to the Congress and to other researchers for consultation, as is the current "Indice de la prensa chilena." The Commission has proposed publication, either on a bimonthly or quarterly basis, with annual cumulations. Possible computerization is being discussed.

Chilean leaders are becoming increasingly convinced that the country needs to develop its technical and scientific capabilities if it is to make the progress toward which it aspires along social, economic, and scientific lines. Various organizations are working toward this end. The phase of the situation which concerns us here is the emerging realization of the need for national bibliographic records of what has been done in the past and what different governmental or university groups or other individuals or organizations are doing currently as a prerequisite for intelligent planning.

Various alphabetical agencies have begun to develop programs. In 1968 ODEPLAN, the Oficina de Planifacación Nacional, named a commission to study the situation. The report dated June 18, 1968, is an important document. (Informe No. 1 de la Comisión Asesora en Documentación de

ODEPLAN. Santiago de Chile, 18 de junio 1968.) It analyzes the situation, indicating that there are great needs but also that there is at present much overlapping of function and records. It concludes by recommending the creation of a national coordinating center for information and documentation, to function under the Comisión Científica y Tecnológica and in cooperation with the Consejo de Rectores. The agency which has been charged with responsibility for implementing the program is CENID, the Centro Nacional de Información y Documentación, currently headed by Mrs. Betty Johnson.

The duties of the coordinating center as outlined in the commission report include: (1) analyzing of existing information, such as archives, indexes, and special studies; (2) establishing systems, whether manual or mechanized, for locating desired information; (3) maintaining informational sources for providing data to national researchers or to those in other countries; and (4) coordinating the operation of existing libraries and centers and maintaining international relations which assure the acquisition of information from throughout the world.

The expressed hopes of ODEPLAN that the necessary preliminaries, such as budget and other estimates, could be carried out in 1969 and the program could get under way by 1970 seem to be well on their way to realization. Mrs. Johnson indicated in a conversation, May, 1969, that bibliography is considered one of the incidental objectives, a means towards an end. Although scientific and technical considerations are paramount, the terms under which CENID functions are interpreted liberally, and some assistance can be given to materials in the humanities and social sciences. Also, the Biblioteca Nacional will be encouraged to direct its indexing activities where possible towards current social science materials rather than retrospective literature. In any case it seems that major official developments are in the offing concerning the acquiring, recording, and making available of information concerning Chile's more important current national bibliographical output.

An unrelated development which may yield more immediate and general results in terms of current national bibliography can also be reported. Sr. Zamorano y Caperán, whose *Servicio bibliográfico chileno* (1940–) has supplied the only consistent record of Chilean publications for three decades, has agreed to include in his quarterly lists, which are prepared primarily for his foreign clientele, the names of the publishers. This addition makes possible the use of his lists by the *Fichero bibliográfico hispanoamericano*, which will in turn make available an author listing as well as a classified one, and will provide for an extension of the usefulness of the data through inclusion in *Libros en venta.* Sr. Zamorano y Caperán estimates that his lists include 90 percent of the more substantial book production of Santiago, and he states that very little is produced elsewhere.

Summary

Chile, as the homeland of José Toribio Medina, is heir to the most outstanding bibliographic tradition of the Americas, which has been carried on to a considerable extent through Don Guillermo Feliú Cruz. A major achievement of the latter was the updating of the *Anuario de la prensa chilena,* an author listing of publications reaching the Biblioteca Nacional. The record is being continued, although at present on a biennial basis. The major source of current information continues to be the quarterly *Servicio bibliográfico chileno,* a bookdealer's list.

New developments in the bibliographic arts in Chile are along lines designed to meet immediate needs for economic and political data, notably: (1) plans for the creation of a national coordinating center for information and documentation to be responsible to CENID, the Centro Nacional de Información y Documentación, and (2) an expanded program for the indexing of Chilean newspapers by the national Library of Congress.

COLOMBIA

Startling geographic contrasts in Colombia and corresponding problems in communication are reflected in the country's bibliographic records, but recent decades have brought dramatic changes. Before the airplane completely revolutionized transportation, the three Andean ranges extending from the country's southern border toward the north had blocked east-west communications. Life flowed from south to north, along the valleys of the Cauca and the Magdalena rivers. The journey to Bogotá, using river steamers up the Magdalena until halted by rapids, then continuing by train, took at least a week. Bogotá, founded in 1538, was an Archbishopric, which became the center of the Viceroyalty of New Granada. It came to be called the "Athens of America," a title it prized highly.

In most other Latin American countries, the capital is the principal city and publishing center of the country, but Bogotá has had exceptional competition. The air age has enhanced the relative position of the capital, which now has a population of some two million. But Medellín, approaching its first million, Cali well on its way towards that number, Barranquilla past the half-way mark, and the port cities of Bucaramanga and Cartagena past the quarter point, are all important cities in their own right. The diversity is reflected in the existence of regional historical or other cultural journals, of which the Zimmerman *Guide to Current Latin American Periodicals* (1961), listed twelve currently published as of 1960. In terms of present-day local bibliography, the first four cities named were all represented in the *Fichero bibliográfico hispanoamericano's* list of contributing publishers in a typical issue (March 1969). Many countries with only one real publishing center complain that compliance with the law of legal deposit is poor. In Colombia (where the law calls for the deposit of copies of all works in the National Library) that country's repeated complaint of noncompliance may be exceptionally well based.

Given the existing geographical and historical circumstances, the lack of a bibliographical tradition in Colombia is understandable. Recently, however, the country, with its internal communications vastly improved by air transportation, has made great efforts to develop and maintain adequate bibliographical records, and its progress has been remarkable. In a paper entitled "Colombian Bibliography" written by Rubén Pérez Ortiz for the Sixth Seminar (1961), he stated that concern over the establishment of bibliographical services in Colombia began with a paper which he prepared for UNESCO in 1950 entitled "Improvement of Bibliographic Service." He noted that credit was due UNESCO and the Organization of American States for providing the initial stimulus for such progress as had been made. He considered such stimulus a service which international organizations could and should render to countries "when there is no clear knowledge of what . . . bibliography represents to the cultural and material advancement of their people."

When Rubén Pérez Ortiz wrote his 1961 account of the state of Colombian bibliography, he had become the Head of the Bibliographic Department of the Instituto Caro y Cuervo,* an Institute which had long enjoyed an international reputation for its work on linguistics and in bibliography related to that field, but which had only recently undertaken responsibility for compiling and publishing the current national bibliography.

The first *Anuario bibliográfico colombiano* was compiled by Pedro R.

---

* An article by Guillermo de Zéndegui, "Temple of the Spanish Language," in *Américas* for January 1964, gives an excellent account of the Institute, with illustrations showing its Hacienda Yerbabuena setting and its Director, José Manuel Rivas Sacconi. The ICC has an office in the National Library, but its files for national bibliography, current and retrospective, are maintained on the Yerbabuena premises.

Carmona and was published in Cali in 1951. Its contents were incorporated into the next volume, 1951/1956. This was compiled by Rubén Pérez Ortiz, as were subsequent volumes through 1962. The 1963 volume, published in 1966, was entitled *Anuario bibliográfico colombiano "Rubén Pérez Ortiz."* In the preface the new editor, Francisco José Romero Rojas, paid tribute to his predecessor, who died in April 1964. He reviewed briefly the publishing history of the *Anuario* and stated that it would continue along previous lines. Books and pamphlets would be listed on the basis of the Dewey Decimal System, and a comprehensive index of names would be provided. Annual lists of new periodicals were also to be continued. Dr. Romero Rojas thanked those who had cooperated in supplying data or in allowing their collections to be checked. However, he urged fuller compliance in the national interest with Decree Number 2840, dated November 14, 1961, and signed by the President and the Minister of National Education.

This rather remarkable document stated that in accordance with a 1954 decree the Instituto Caro y Cuervo had been charged with the compiling of the national bibliography and that a Department of Bibliography had been created for the purpose. It was therefore decreed that all publishers should send a copy of every item printed by them to the Instituto Caro y Cuervo within one month of its publication date. It was provided that in the case of noncommercial items they might be loaned to the Institute with a written request that they be returned when bibliographic data had been noted for the *Anuario*. Compliance was asked for, but no penalty was indicated for failure to send the materials. Even though the supposed requirement may be less than fully effective, the intent and language of the decree, signed by a President of international stature—Alberto Lleras Camargo, a former Secretary-General of the OAS —gave new prestige to the concept of national bibliography in Colombia, and by extension throughout Latin America: Considering "That it is the duty of government to support every effort which makes for the diffusion of the intellectual patrimony of Colombians and that the compilation and publication of bibliographies is the most practical means of making known the contribution of Colombia to sciences, arts, and letters. . . ."*

In spite of difficulties the ICC's Department of Bibliography has succeeded in bringing the *Anuario* up to date. Dr. Romero Rojas stated to this writer in May 1969 that the 1967/1968 volume was then in press and that it was his intention to maintain a current publishing schedule. Publications

* Translation by this writer. The decree is included in some issues of the *Anuario*, e.g., 1962 and 1964/1965, with the unnumbered pages following the index.

which reached him tardily (and only items personally handled by him were included) would be listed later. Work on a 1951 to 1968 supplement was in progress, but no target date had been set for its completion. He reported that the compliance of publishers with the 1961 decree was improving but that it was not yet good. The 1967/1968 volume did in fact appear in 1969. The 349-page volume bears a colophon date of September 5, 1969. The achievement is a landmark in the history of Colombia's national bibliography and is a cause for hearty congratulations.

The effects of the 1950 UNESCO Conference on the Improvement of Bibliographic Services on Rubén Pérez Ortiz and through him on Colombian national bibliography have been noted. Colombia proved to be doubly benefited, since the early 1960s brought it the services of another distinguished participant at that conference, Dr. Fermín Peraza. Dr. Peraza and his wife had departed Castro's Cuba in late 1960 to serve in the Escuela Interamericana de Bibliotecología, where they remained until early in 1962. While in Medellín, Dr. Peraza compiled and published, as a part of the series "Biblioteca del bibliotecario," *Fichas para el Anuario bibliográfico colombiano,* with a special section for "Libros de Medellín." This section was dropped when the Perazas left Medellín for Gainesville, Florida, in 1962 to join the staff of the University of Florida Libraries. The title was changed in 1965 to *Bibliografía colombiana.* The Peraza approach covered books and pamphlets published in Colombia or by Colombians living elsewhere and foreign materials dealing with Colombia. Official publications were included on a rather extensive basis. Arrangement was alphabetical by author with a detailed subject index.*

Colombian national bibliography advanced during the 1960s in a specific area which has been generally neglected in Latin America—the listing of official publications. In 1964 the Escuela Interamericana de Bibliotecología in Medellín published the first issue of *Bibliografía oficial colombiana.* It listed publications of national, departmental (state), municipal, and autonomous agencies. Number 2 appeared in 1966. A "Presentación" (pp. iii-v), by Florén Lozano, head of the editorial board, indicated the difficulties encountered in preparing the *Bibliografías,* but intentions of quarterly publishing and of providing an annual cumulated volume were expressed. The title is included in the EIB's *Lista de publicaciones para la venta,* updated to March 1969. It was hoped to have a recent copy at hand, but international mail problems prevented the realization of the hope.

---

* For a more detailed description of both the *Anuario bibliográfico colombiano "Rubén Pérez Ortiz"* and *Bibliografía colombiana* see Peraza's *Bibliografías corrientes de la América Latina, 1969,* pp. 45-46.

The *Bibliografía oficial colombiana* had its origins apparently in two papers prepared respectively by Fermín Peraza and José Ignacio Bohórquez for the Conferencia sobre Administración Pública en los Países en Desarrollo, Bogotá, April 15-21, 1963. The Peraza paper was entitled "Publicaciones oficiales colombianas, 1961-1962," and the one by Bohórquez was a "Lista de las publicaciones hechas por la Imprenta Nacional de Colombia, 1958-1962." The two papers were published in 1964 by Peraza under the title of *Publicaciones oficiales colombianas* in his series "Biblioteca del bibliotecario" (no. 69). The foreword stated that the papers, prepared for the April 1963 Conference, had been distributed in such a limited edition that it had seemed desirable to make them more widely available. Sr. Bohórquez has continued to work with official publications. He contributed to the Eleventh Seminar (1966) an extensive "Lista alfabética de las entidades de la administración pública nacional de Colombia, 1821-1966."

Mention should be made of the contributions to special phases of Colombian national bibliography made by the Director of, or by students in, the UNESCO- and foundation-sponsored Escuela Interamericana de Bibliotecología, which is now a part of the University of Antioquia in Medellín. Of the list of publications for sale as of March 1969 several were dated as recently as 1967, and the following three either specifically covered through 1967 or were dated 1968:

Florén Lozano, Luis. *Obras de referencia y generales de la bibliografía colombiana.* Medellín, Editorial Universidad de Antioquia, 1968. 226 leaves. Mimeo.

Lorenzo E., Concepción Pablo. *Repertorio de las publicaciones corrientes colombianas,* 1960–1968. Medellín, EUA, 1968. 180 leaves. Mimeo.

Lotero Marín, Libia. *Indice científico y técnico colombiano 1964–1967.* Medellín, EUA, 1968. 148 leaves. Mimeo.*

There are several other *índices* compiled by various students as of their respective years of graduation. In some cases work carried to a certain date is continued later. An undated circular available as of May 1969 listed, in addition to the *Indice* noted above, an *Indice agrícola colombiano, 1951-1960*, the same for 1961-1966, an *Indice antioqueño de educación, 1871-1965*, an *Indice económico colombiano, 1960-1966* (continuing an earlier one for 1951-1960), an *Indice militar colombiano* (1955-1967), and an *Indice odontológico colombiano* (1887-1966.) The Director himself, Luis Florén Lozano, has published *Bibliografía bibliotecológica colom-*

---

* The three publications are available from the Editorial Universidad de Antioquia, Medellín, Colombia, at U.S. $25.00, $30.00, and $30.00 respectively.

biana, first up to 1960, additional lists for 1963 and 1964, and in 1967 a five-year cumulative list. The series will presumably continue.

The 1968/1969 *Anuario bibliográfico* lists also, with the Escuela as author, a *Lista de publicaciones periódicas y en serie; actualizado al mes de agosto de 1968,* published by the Editorial Universidad de Antioquia in 1968.

Further information concerning Colombian periodicals comes from an unlikely source, the División de Información y Publicaciones of the Departamento Administrativo Nacional de Estadística. One reference to its *Publicaciones periódicas en Colombia* as an annual has been noted, but a belated effort to learn whether there have been other editions than the one at hand, with data for 1965 but published in 1967, has not as yet been successful. In this record the basic treatment is, as would be expected, statistical. Charts show a breakdown of the 408 titles treated, first as to their periodicity and next by type—scientific, literary, sports, etc. Most of the bulletin (pages 10-62), however, is devoted to an alphabetical listing by province and town of individual titles, with addresses. Only the kind (agricultural, tourist, etc.) and periodicity of each are noted.

Summary

Colombia, in spite of a strong cultural tradition, lacked anything resembling an *anuario* until after 1950, when Rubén Pérez Ortiz presented a paper at a UNESCO Conference on the "Improvement of Bibliographic Service." He credited UNESCO and the OAS with providing the stimulus which led to the initial compilation of an *anuario* and for encouraging its continuation. Since his death it is being prepared by a former associate of Pérez Ortiz, Dr. Francisco J. Romero Rojas, whose bibliographic work is supported by the Instituto Caro y Cuervo. With the publication in 1969 of the 1967/1968 volume of the *Anuario bibliográfico colombiano "Rubén Pérez Ortiz,"* Colombia's national bibliography has achieved currency and can be expected to maintain its schedule. Colombia has within two decades moved from the category of countries with no history of real national bibliography to the ranks of the most advanced, both as to quality and as to current publication.

Colombia benefits also from the bibliographical works produced by students and faculty of the Escuela Interamericana de Bibliotecología in Medellín, which provide bibliographies on specific aspects of national publications. Some of these compilations cover their materials to the date of their publication.

ECUADOR

Ecuador provides inadequate information about such publishing as is done within its borders, but both the publishing and its record have distinctive characteristics. A report on Ecuador in the UNESCO bulletin *Bibliography, Documentation, and Terminology* for May 1968 says in part:

> There are two main publishing houses in Quito: the Casa de la Cultura Ecuatoriana and the Editorial Universitaria, which is attached to the Universidad Central. . . . The Editorial Universitaria keeps a very brief catalog of the works it offers for sale; it has no catalog of books published in recent years.
>
> The Casa de la Cultura Ecuatoriana is the only institution which has been publishing since its creation (August, 1944) a bibliographical catalog of the works by Ecuadorian authors. Special mention should be made of the work entitled: *20 años de labor de la Casa de Cultura Ecuatoriana* which lists 444 authors.

This catalog, cited above by its cover title, is officially a *Catálogo general de publicaciones de la Casa de la Cultura Ecuatoriana, 1944-1965,* published in 1965 by the Casa.* This 230-page volume (on good paper) is indeed a valuable record. Arranged basically by the Dewey Decimal major divisions, it lists chronologically each of the pertinent publications. Most titles are annotated, and portraits accompany many of them. The introduction notes that in many cases the books are ones which are "reappearing." "Editions" are indicated, but these may include reprints, since the distinction in Latin America is not carefully drawn. An alphabetical name index facilitates location of works by specific authors.

One of the distinctive features of the work of the Casa is that while the principal center, the "Casa matriz," is in Quito, there are others, called *núcleos,* elsewhere in the country. In the 20-year catalog of the Casa pages 181-219 are devoted to the publications of the *núcleos.* Those of Guayas and Azuay are listed separately, and seven additional ones are covered in a section on "others."

An earlier catalog, *Libros publicados por la Editorial de la Casa Matriz,* dated 1959, was simply a title-author list (on newsprint) arranged by years, from the four publications in 1945 through the thirty-eight for 1959. The Editorial publishes an annual *Catálogo* regularly and quite

---

* An account of this remarkable organization is to be found in an article by Lilo Linke, "House of Culture: What the Ten-year-old Casa de la Cultura Has Done for the Arts and Sciences in Ecuador," in *Américas* for July 1954 (Vol. 6, pp. 13-15, 41-42).

promptly. However, these too are only title-author price lists arranged in very general groups by type of work, and completely lacking in other bibliographic detail.

The *Catálogo* covering 1944-1965, on the other hand, was the work of Alfredo Chaves, Director of the Archivo Nacional de Historia until his death in 1963, and of Laura de Crespo, Librarian in charge of the Casa's library, which includes the Archivo de la Cultura and attempts to keep copies of all publications of the Editorial. The two were working direct from the publications so far as those were available, and their data were accurate and complete. The *Catálogo* is important not only for itself but because it sets a high standard for Ecuadorian bibliography, national or other.

Emphasis on the publication of *Revistas* is another of the distinguishing characteristics of the work of the Casa de la Cultura Ecuatoriana. Although its own *Revista* suspended publication about 1957, various of the provincial *núcleos* were publishing theirs as recently as the mid-1960s, as reported in *20 años de labor*. Specialized periodicals dealing with such fields as education, literature, and medicine are published by their respective agencies, all apparently affiliated more or less closely with the Casa. The introduction to the cumulated volume for 1944-1965 mentioned these periodicals as an important part of the work of the Casa as publisher.

The dearth of qualified bibliographers and librarians in Ecuador was indicated by the Secretary of the National Library in the 1968 report cited above. He stated that as of 1966 there were no certified librarians in the country, but noted that an Escuela de Bibliotecología had recently been created at the Universidad de Guayaquil. A later report points up further the lack of adequately educated and technically trained librarians in Ecuador. Eleanor Mitchell, who served from 1963 to 1968 as a Saint Louis University/USAID library consultant at the Universidad Católica del Ecuador in Quito, provided an account of developments during those five years in an article, "Pilot Project in the Andes" in the *Library Journal* for November 15, 1968.

As a pilot project should do, the Ecuadorian experiment serves as a more or less representative case study. A country with a low literacy rate will not be book oriented. The possibilities provided by libraries, as made possible by librarians, are not comprehended. Adequate library training is not, under such circumstances, ordinarily available in the home country. Students sent to a center which provides such training—in this case, probably, the Inter-American Library School in Medellín, Colombia—are upon their return in short supply and are highly mobile. It is possible that in such a situation, as noted by Miss Mitchell, the coming or going of one professional librarian can increase or decrease their number in the country by 50 percent!

Two of Miss Mitchell's staff members at the Universidad Católica del Ecuador, Alfredo Alvear and Ximena Espinosa, prepared under her supervision a working paper for the Eleventh Seminar (1966). The paper, "Ecuador, apuntes bibliográficos," is valuable for (1) a sketch of the history of printing in Ecuador, (2) for a good statement of the difficulties encountered by authors and the book trade in general in most Latin American countries, and (3) for information about retrospective Ecuadorian bibliography. However, data about current national bibliography were lacking.

The Ecuadorian situation is one in which the National Library has been in no position to provide bibliographical records or leadership. Eleanor Mitchell stated that the building in which it had functioned for a number of years was a former skating rink, and that its collections and services were limited. However, when she wrote her article in 1968 new quarters were under construction.

The report in *Bibliography, Documentation, and Terminology* for May 1968 (but with 1966 data) stated that the National Library had very limited funds but would gladly cooperate so far as possible with other libraries in Ecuador or elsewhere. There was a law of legal deposit, promulgated in 1934, requiring authors and publishers to send a copy of every work not only to the National Library but to each of three other places—the municipal library of the author's place of residence, to the Biblioteca de Autores Nacionales in Ambato, and to the Municipal Library of Guayaquil.

Hopes for a current bibliographical record were raised briefly by the appearance of a *Boletín bibliográfico ecuatoriano* early in 1967. The *Handbook of Latin American Studies* for 1967 described the January/March issue thus: "A much-needed and welcome source of information. This first issue contains a section on current books and pamphlets." The second issue (dated April/June), an attractively printed one, from the Casa de la Cultura press, devoted most of its twenty-two pages to bibliographical lists, the rest mainly to news notes and a brief article on the library of the Universidad Central. The major section, "Libros y folletos ecuatorianos," evidently continued the listing from the first issue. Items were numbered from 64 through 130. Full bibliographical data showed that the majority were pamphlets, mostly from universities and the Casa de Cultura, including the *núcleos* in the provinces, and other official sources. However, a fair number of "books" (of over one hundred pages) were listed, and some private presses were represented. An "Hemeroteca ecuatoriana," an alphabetical list of 26 Ecuadorian periodicals, with publishing agency and number and date of the latest issue noted—chiefly 1967 publications—was a useful feature.

Unfortunately the *Boletín bibliográfico ecuatoriano* neglected to furnish data as to certain important details—coverage, sponsorship, and availability. No indication was given as to what access to materials had been available, nor was there an estimate as to how complete the record was considered to be. It was "Editado por Alfredo Alvear, Matilde Altimarano, Ximena Espinosa, and Mary Altimarano." Of the four "Editors," Alvear and Espinosa have already been identified as authors of the SALALM working paper on Ecuador, and they mentioned Matilde Altimarano as the Librarian of the Universidad Central in Quito. A post office box number was given, but there was no indication as to terms on which the "quarterly publication" could be secured. An attempt by the University of Florida Libraries to place a subscription brought no reply. "Reliable sources" have established the fact that only two issues were published. At least, those small bulletins provide useful information, and their content and arrangement set an excellent standard for future publications.

On the other hand, the episode does point up several important factors involved in the providing of national bibliography. Internal and supplementary evidence, including "grapevine intelligence," do identify the editors as well-intentioned young librarians who undertook to compile and present the information on their own time, without institutional support and without adequate working capital. For their good intentions, for their considerable effort, and for their contribution to knowledge, they should be given full credit. However, in general terms, there is a negative side to the situation. A few generalizations based on this episode have wide applicability.

1. Any new periodical publication should provide—as many do—a statement as to the identity of the editors and publishers, indicating their objectives, their sponsorship, the intended periodicity of the publication, and the terms upon which it may be secured.

2. Serial publications, which involve the setting up of an "open entry" as a sort of birth certificate, are presumed still to be published until definite information—preferably an official notice—provides a "death certificate." Until the latter is recorded, a fantastic total of hours of staff time in American and other libraries can be spent in attempting to secure the

publication or to ascertain its status. The greater the prestige and circulation of the bibliographic tools carrying the original entry, such as the *Handbook of Latin American Studies* and *New Serial Titles,* the greater the responsibility for providing adequate data.

3. Any serial publication should provide specific information as to the source from which it can be obtained. Subscription price or terms of exchange should be clearly stated.

4. Monographic publications which provide information of a given date can be landmarks as such. If the group which assembles the information is of an ephemeral nature, it is a more professional procedure to provide a single dated pamphlet or book than to launch a periodical which will soon be orphaned. If supplements prove feasible, they can be provided. If a periodical should later emerge, given a solid working basis, good. In any case, "responsible parenthood" will avoid contributing to a population explosion in short-lived periodicals, which strew the records of Latin American periodicals. Too many such corpses lack "death certificates," and have not, therefore, been given "decent burial."

Bibliographic information from commercial sources concerning Ecuadorian publications is understandably scarce. Even such data as are provided by the annual catalogs of the Casa de Cultura are deplorably incomplete, a fact necessarily reflected in any use *Fichero* might attempt to make of that basic source. What information *Comentarios bibliográficos americanos* may be able to provide remains to be seen. At present the Stechert-Hafner LACAP lists are among the better sources, together with those from Latin American dealers who provide bibliographically acceptable lists from other countries more or less frequently, notably E. Iturriaga in Lima. Those of Fernando García Cambeiro in Buenos Aires are often excellent but are somewhat variable.

Summary

Ecuador has a low level of book consciousness with a correspondingly low level of publishing and of demands for libraries and for bibliographical services. Most of the publications issued in the country are sponsored by the universities, especially the Universidad Central, or by the Casa de la Cultura Ecuatoriana. The latter, the country's chief publisher, provides the only regular and reasonably current source of information concerning publishing in Ecuador through its own annual catalogs, but they are deficient in bibliographic information.

Ecuador received significant assistance towards library development from international agencies in the 1960s through the provision of outstanding professional personnel in a leadership capacity and through opportunities offered to young recruits to the profession. New library and bibliographical standards were set, and there were indications that the seed planted might be fruitful. The two issues of the "quarterly" *Boletín bibliográfico ecuatoriano,* dated for the first half of 1967, provided valuable information as of that date and set some excellent standards.

PARAGUAY

Paraguay was one of the countries to which the Ninth Seminar (1964) gave special attention. Mrs. Mary Brennan, of the Order Department of the University of Texas Library, wrote on "Library Resources and Acquisitions," and Sofía Mareski, Librarian of the National Administration of Telecommunications' Institute of Telecommunications, contributed "The Present Situation of Book Publication: Means of Production, Exchange of Publications, List of Official Organizations, and Bibliography of Official Periodical Publications." No attempt was made to treat specifically national bibliography, current or retrospective, perhaps because there was so little to say.

Mrs. Brennan, who had sent out a questionnaire, felt that there were so many qualifications attached to the 39 replies received that any statements made should be hedged by "a private *más o menos.*" However, she provided some interesting facts and comments. Bibliographic tools used in acquiring current materials concerning Paraguay, as reported by the questionnaires, were "the generally familiar ones." Of the nonspecific tools, "publishers' and dealers' catalogs," with 14, was nearly double any other source. Of 11 specific sources used, the top 5 were: *Fichero bibliográfico hispanoamericano,* 17; Pan American Union, Columbus Memorial Library, *List of Books Accessioned . . .,* 8; *National Union Catalog,* 7; *Revista interamericana de bibliografía,* 7; Stechert-Hafner lists (LACAP), 7.

With regard to exchange programs, only 17 of the 39 questionnaires returned marked this section in any way. Of these, few had dealt with more than one or two institutions, namely: Library of Congress, 16; University of Florida, 8; University of Texas, 7; Pan American Health Organization, 6; University of California, Berkeley, 4. Principal difficulties at the Paraguayan end were considered to be the extreme degree of decentralization in government agencies and academic institutions. In the

United States hampering factors were lack of staff and of publications to offer in exchange.

One section has so much application to other Latin American countries, as well as Paraguay, that it merits quotation in full:

V. A recitation of the problems surrounding Latin American acquisitions makes a doleful dirge indeed. In the order of diminishing emphasis, these are the problems:
   1. Lack of reliable, up-to-date bibliographies
   2. Lack of reliable dealers
   3. Failure to elicit replies to correspondence
   4. Difficulty in obtaining government documents
   5. Decentralization of academic and government agencies
   6. Refusal to accept standing orders
   7. Necessity of prepayment
   8. Inadequate printings
   9. High prices
   10. Lack of interest here in the United States

The suggested solutions, some well within the realm of possibility, some not, are the following:

   1. Improved exchange programs
   2. Larger printings
   3. Greater academic and government centralization
   4. Better organized book trade in Latin America
   5. National agencies patterned after Her Majesty's Stationary Office

The section of the paper by the Paraguayan librarian, Sofía Mareski, which deals with "Exchange of Publications in Paraguay and Abroad" is of particular interest when viewed conversely to the foregoing presentation as a statement of the difficulties encountered at the southern end of the line.

The exchange of official publications in Paraguay takes place more inside the country, among Ministries and institutions, than outside. There are very few Ministries or institutions who keep an exchange service with the outside because of the following reasons:

   1. According to the information received from some ministries there is no provision in the budget for mailing costs. This problem is solved locally by the use of messengers.
   2. Another obstacle is the language factor involving correspond-

ence regarding requests, receipts, and other information of
that nature.

3. There are very few Ministries that have a library, or if they do
   it does not accomplish this task because of the lack of
   professional librarians; the exchange is a specific library task.
   Generally, the Publications Departments do not distribute
   their own publications; it is usually done by the Public
   Relations offices and secretaries.

Miss Mareski stated that the Library of the National Administration of
Telecommunications (her post) maintained a good exchange service with
five continents on the basis of two bulletins available to it free of charge
for this purpose. Its statistical bulletin, which had "a circulation of 200
issues," was mailed to 103 centers in the different continents. *Teleinforma-
tivo,* with a circulation of 1,000 copies, was distributed among executives
of local private enterprises and a small number to the same abroad. She
considered the exchange as advantageous to her library, but she mentioned
regretfully the cancellation of the contract with the United States Book
Exchange, which, "according to correspondence received through USAID
in Paraguay was done because of the reduction in foreign aid. But since
they expressed, though, that they would like to continue receiving our
publications, we have decided to keep them on our mailing list."

The withdrawal of the AID subsidy (primarily a matter of transportation costs) was a decision which compelled the USBE to cancel without
warning its contracts with Latin American countries. The cancellation of
the subsidy was particularly disastrous in situations such as that of Paraguay, a country which is almost a complete void in bibliographical terms.
The fact that USBE had been able to secure from the country publications
whose existence might otherwise be unknown and could make them
available to its customers at cost, by means of its lists, was highly
advantageous. Since USBE lists are prepared with publications in hand, the
bibliographic data can be relied upon for completeness and accuracy. The
USBE program is still important, but it can no longer make available the
quantity or quality of materials from places such as Paraguay which its
lists formerly offered.

One of the useful features of the Mareski paper was the appendices: a
list of official agencies and a list of official periodical publications. The
special importance of government documents, as the chief publications
produced in the country, pointed up particular difficulties in the production of any type of book materials in Paraguay. An obvious limitation was
the geographical factor of proximity to the publishing centers of Argentina

and Brazil. Another was heavy customs duties and taxes on the materials and equipment required for printing, which made it less expensive to import the finished publications themselves. A third limitation—one common to most of the less developed countries—was a lack of artisans with the required skills for printing and binding. Since government agencies were exempt from the levies of duties and taxes, they had a great advantage over private enterprise.

A section on existing facilities for the printing and reproduction of books (which bears on the question, what *is* a "publication"?) listed them in two categories: (1) Private enterprise—publications of the "40 graphic establishments in the country," mostly mimeographed and stapled ("Almost all the colleges, schools, offices, and private firms have a mimeograph"); (2) governmental—a detailed listing of the mimeographing or other means of reproducing "printed matter." A "lynotype, model 31, and a disc type ruling press" listed for the National Printing Office put it far in the lead. There is no mention that any one of the agencies keeps any kind of record of what comes from its rollers or presses.

It seems clear that the reasons for a lack of national bibliography lie deep indeed. There is a new National Library building, but as an institution it is, at best, not expressing leadership.*

As in other national situations, the more difficult the publication of books, the greater the role of official bulletins or reviews and of those published independently or by societies. The two SALALM papers both present useful information regarding Paraguayan periodicals in their respective appendices. Mareski provides as "Anexo 2" a list of ten ministries and periodicals published by them. An apology for its incompleteness, due to a lack of time for its compilation, is itself an indication of the lack of bibliographical resources at her command.

The Brennan paper provides a list, "Periodicals Currently Received from Paraguay" (Appendix 2). This appendix, with data compiled from a variety of sources, including questionnaires and the *Union List of Serials* and *New Serial Titles 1961-1962,* provides useful information of two kinds. First is a list of 35 institutions in the United States and Canada "which have indicated they currently receive the periodicals (or hope they do)." Of the 35 libraries, the only ones indicating the current receipt of

---

* Mrs. Rosa Q. Mesa, Latin American Documents Librarian at the University of Florida, reports that on the occasion of her visit to Paraguay in March 1969 she went twice to the new Biblioteca Nacional but found only a caretaker on duty. According to her Paraguayan contacts, the move to the new building had been considered an opportunity to do some housecleaning, and only the better looking materials had been transferred.

more than 5 titles were the following: Library of Congress, 41; New York Public Library, 16; University of Texas, 13; Pan American Union, 10; University of Florida, 10; University of California, Berkeley, 9; and the Department of State Library, 6. The second part of the list is, in fact, a union list of current Paraguayan periodicals based upon the sources indicated. It merits wider availability than is offered by its appendix status.

Under the circumstances described, the bookdealer substitutes to some extent for the bibliographer. The best known bookdealer in Paraguay is the Agencia de Librerías Nizza, S.A., in Asunción. The bookstore is reported to be well organized, and it distributes a price list, "Bibliografía paraguaya," at unstated intervals. Another dealer who prepares occasional lists of books by Paraguayan authors and of books about Paraguay is the Librería Juan de Salazar. However, the two seen by this writer were unpaged, and items were neither numbered nor alphabetized. A third Paraguayan firm, the Librería Comuneros, ordinarily sends out general lists of Latin American materials. However, the proprietor, Ricardo Rolón, did prepare on request a list of Paraguayan documents in January 1969, and he might prepare other catalogs of Paraguayan materials. His lists are well presented and provide full data except for publisher.

Such sources at best, however, supply only a limited amount of unorganized information, with scant offerings of current publications. As elsewhere, the providing of such data as are available about current publications to *Fichero bibliográfico hispanoamericano* for use there and in *Libros en venta* would make the information more nearly available as current national bibliography. The same may prove true for the new *Comentarios bibliográficos americanos* and its proposed annual cumulation.

Once the information is available in some form, it is always possible that a bibliographer may appear to convert the raw data into an organized bibliography. The chances for this eventuality have been increased by the instituting recently of the University of Paraguay's School of Library Sciences under the direction of Dr. Gastón Litton.

Summary

Paraguay seems to concentrate in one spot most of the difficulties of the Latin American book world in the production of books and in providing adequate bibliographical information about what does get published currently. In the absence of bibliographical sources as such, we are largely dependent upon dealers for information, provided either directly or through commercially produced international bibliographies.

PERU

Peru's coverage of its national bibliography may well be the most nearly complete of that of any Latin American country. Its *Anuario bibliográfico peruano* (1943-), which now holds the longevity record among its kind, began publication within a few months after the fire which destroyed the National Library in May 1943. Much of the manuscript and other materials were tragically irreplaceable, but library officials, notably Alberto Tauro and Jorge Basadre, requested and received international cooperation in the rebuilding of a Peruvian collection and in its organization. One of the various constructive results was the establishment of an extensive and well-organized system of bibliographic coverage.

The *Anuario* provides a classified list of Peruvian books and pamphlets published within the years covered and also a separate listing by agencies of official publications, supplemented by a list of foreign publications concerning Peru. An author index covering the relevant years is provided. The listing of periodicals is exceptionally complete and well organized. Classified listings of periodicals published in Lima and in the provinces are given with full data, including the numbers and dates of issues published during the period, or at least of the most recent issue received by the library. Similar treatment is given official serial publications. A comprehensive title index covers both sections.

"Biobibliografías de peruanos desaparecidos" is given only one line in the table of contents, but the detailed data are awarded what may be a disproportionately large amount of space. In the 1958/60 volume, for instance, the national bibliography, as listed above, covered pages 1-431, and "Biobibliografías de escritores peruanos desaparecidos en los años 1958-1960" took up pages 433-743. To the extent that the labor and costs of providing such personal data, even for outstanding writers, may infringe upon the possibilities of prompt publication of the current national bibliography, the devotion of so much space to them in the *Anuario* seems of dubious justification. Inclusion in the Library's *Boletín* or in its review, *Fénix*, would seem more appropriate.

The *Anuario* fell several years behind date in the 1950s, but the Library has made a strenuous effort to achieve currency. A volume covering 1958/60 was published in 1964 and one for 1961/63, the twentieth anniversary number, is dated 1966 on the title page but bears a colophon date of December 11, 1967. The Library's *Memoria* for 1962/66, published in 1967, stated that the *Anuario* for 1964/66 would be published in 1967. Apparently a delay in publication occurred, but at least the Library had fulfilled its responsibilities for compilation of the data. That fact is a cause for congratulation.

The quarterly *Boletín de la Biblioteca Nacional,* which also dates from 1943, carries a classified list of recent publications, with full bibliographic data but without an author index. There are periodic lists of copyright entries, arranged on a daily basis, with names in signature form and with no index. The bibliographic value of such a listing is scant, if not nil. The *Boletín* is currently received by United States libraries up to two years or so behind date.

Peru may claim not only the oldest current *Anuario* of Latin America but also the dean of university bibliographic bulletins and one which in most of its sister republics would have been the country's principal source of national bibliography for nearly half a century. Fittingly enough, it is the *Boletín bibliográfico,* organ of the Biblioteca Central de la Universidad Nacional Mayor de San Marcos, which is the oldest and best of such publications. Founded in 1923, it has been published continuously except for the period January 1930 to October 1934. It is numbered as a quarterly but of recent years has usually appeared on a semestral or annual basis.

The *Boletín bibliográfico* publishes a classified list of the books and pamphlets received by the University's Central Library, complete with author index. Its most distinctive contribution to the current national bibliography, however, is the selective, classified index to periodical articles appearing in the Peruvian journals received, and to some extent to outstanding articles in national newspapers of the period covered. A time lag of two years or more in publication limits the value of the information provided as "current" bibliography but not its later value for research purposes.

Peru is fortunate, bibliographically speaking, in the supplementary information provided by its book trade. There are several Lima firms which publish catalogs of varying quality more or less frequently. Of these, E. Iturriaga & Cía., S.A., has been providing for more than twenty years semiannual catalogs with at least a section devoted to recent Peruvian publications. It was a helpful measure when, beginning not later than mid-1967, Iturriaga began to separate his mimeographed catalog into two parts; the shorter one is a separately numbered list, *Libros recientes.*

Peru was one of the countries considered by the Ninth Seminar (1964), but there was no working paper which dealt specifically with its bibliography. James McShane Breedlove, in his paper on "Library Resources and Acquisitions and Exchange Policies Relating to Peru," was critical of the *Anuario bibliográfico peruano* because of its tardy appearance. In reply to his question, "Which bibliographic tools do you use for current materials? " the leading source was given as "Bookdealers' and publishers' catalogs." The answers to "Which bookdealers do you use for current materials? " were: (1) for the United States, Stechert-Hafner, which led by nearly triple the total for the other five, (2) and for Peru, Iturriaga, with double the total for the other three.

Bettina Summers Pagés, Chief of the Department of Acquisitions of the National Libraries of Peru, contributed a brief paper on "The Publishing Industry in Peru." She stated that the publishing industry was not developed, and that the Cámara del Libro was devoted almost exclusively to the interests of bookdealers. The scant production in the provinces came from the cities of Arequipa, Cuzco, and Trujillo, but there was no bibliographic record even in newspaper advertisements (because of their high prices), and acquisition was therefore a matter of chance. The fact reflects, obviously, the chances that provincial publications would reach the Biblioteca Nacional for inclusion in the *Anuario.*

Breedlove had found *Fichero bibliográfico hispanoamericano* to be the leading specific tool used for the selection of current materials by more than double the number of any other two sources. However, Peru is meagerly represented in *Fichero.* The lack would seem easily remediable by Iturriaga's providing to it periodically the information assembled for his semiannual catalogs, a step which would surely be to their mutual advantage. Potential buyers would benefit immediately, and a bibliographical record would be provided pending the publication of *Libros en venta* and of the *Anuario bibliográfico peruano.* The first two issues of *Comentarios bibliográficos americanos* included several Peruvian firms, notably Mejía Baca listed both as publisher and distributor.

Summary

The Biblioteca Nacional provides excellent coverage in its *Anuario bibliográfico peruano* of all materials acquired by it. However, the *Anuario,* which includes lengthy biobibliographies, appears too late to provide a really current record. The Universidad Nacional Mayor de San Marcos provides a useful supplement to the official record by its *Boletín bibliográfico,* but it too lags behind date. One bookdealer, E. Iturriaga & Cía., S.A., provides, semiannually, reliable and bibliographically excellent lists of recent Peruvian publications. Peru has been poorly represented in *Fichero* but is less so in early issues of *Comentarios bibliográficos americanos.*

URUGUAY

"Book Publishing in Uruguay" was prepared for the Ninth Seminar (1964) by Miguel Angel Piñeiro, a professor of the University Library School of Uruguay, and Luis Alberto Musso, Director of the Technical and Bibliographic Divisions of the Library of the Legislative Power of Uruguay. They provided an excellent account of the past and the current publishing and bibliographical situations as of that date. They noted that, although Uruguay's literary rate was among the highest in Latin America, its book production was low. Geographical location was held largely responsible, since the country is so near to Buenos Aires and is not far from Santiago, both major publishing centers. Other factors mentioned included high costs of materials and labor in an inflationary economy, a relatively small market, and a lack of an efficient system of international distribution.

The authors noted that the National University and the Ministry of Education were both active publishers, and that important books had been produced by them. They stressed a fact—one which is applicable throughout Latin America—that in situations where publication of their works in monographic form is impractical, writers depend heavily upon reviews as an outlet. They added: "Fortunately, also, the organizations already mentioned publish a series of journals of outstanding literary and scientific value to which many of the national authors have contributed with important pieces which otherwise might have never been published" (p. 3).

The *Anuario bibliográfico uruguayo,* published only from 1946 to 1949, was an attempt to compile a national bibliography based on books and pamphlets received on legal deposit by the National Library. Piñeiro and Musso indicated that information from that Library led them to believe that the 1962 and 1963 volumes were to be expected soon, as was also a 1950 volume. It was hoped that a volume covering the years 1951 to 1961 would be published. As of the date of the paper, 1964, the reportedly forthcoming volumes would have brought the national bibliography up to date, but apparently none of the volumes then in preparation has been published.

Bibliografía uruguaya was initiated in 1962 by the Biblioteca del Poder Legislativo as an attempt to produce a record of the current production of Uruguayan nonserial publications. It was first numbered as a quarterly with an annual cumulation in two volumes. However, the two volumes for 1963, published in 1964, were dated as an annual. A small addenda volume for 1963, published in 1966, was the last published as of late 1969.

In the first volume arrangement was alphabetical by author. Annotations were the rule. Bibliographical data included a Dewey Decimal number as an indication of content. In keeping with the declared objectives of making Uruguayan works better known elsewhere, their availability was enhanced by the inclusion not only of publisher but of price. The second volume consisted chiefly of biobibliographies. Both volumes included sections providing information about related matters, such as series, publishers, pseudonyms, and prices.

Bibliografía uruguaya, mimeographed on newsprint, was designed in part for distribution on an exchange basis with the Library's world-wide network of exchange partners. The material represents a great investment in the time of skilled and knowledgeable bibliographers, and the contents are a valuable record. The bibliography served its objectives creditably, and it is to be hoped that its publication can be resumed.

The authors of the SALALM paper noted that since the only institution in the country which was designated as a legal depository was the National Library, the compilation of the national bibliography elsewhere was difficult. As of 1964 they were hoping for the passage of a bill which would extend the privilege to the congressional library as well. Meanwhile, compilation of *Bibliografía uruguaya* was continuing.

Since Uruguay's political and financial problems of the late sixties are well known, it may be supposed that they account for an apparent lack of support, and for the loss to their country and to others of data compiled but not made available in printed form. Uruguay is a country not only of above average literacy for Latin America but also one with even more political and ideological cross currents than the average among its neighbors. Rivalries naturally abound, and as is too commonly true in the Americas, legislative bodies pressed for funds assign a low priority to requests concerning libraries and bibliographies.

Bibliography, Documentation, and Terminology for July 1968 provided among its several national reports a rather full one regarding the situation in Uruguay as of 1966. Nothing was said of updating the *Anuario bibliográfico uruguayo,* but it was stated that the National Library was compiling a retrospective bibliography, with data for 1807-1850 assembled but not yet published. Mention was made of several specialized bibliographies, notably a contribution by Luis Alberto Musso, whose *Bibliografía del Poder Legislativo desde sus comienzos hasta el año 1965* was published by the Cámara de Senadores in 1966.

That Uruguay should have a flourishing book trade is to be expected. The lack of officially produced national bibliography lends added importance to the fact that bookdealers and publishers distribute catalogs which rank them among the top two or three Latin American countries in the supplying of information about their national publications by this method. Some catalogs regularly include sections on reviews, not necessarily devoted exclusively to Uruguayan titles by including them, and are a major source of such information as is available about Uruguayan periodicals. The dearth of information is the more unfortunate because of the wide spectrum of political and social thought reflected in them.

Fichero bibliográfico hispanoamericano listed some twenty Uruguayan publishers or dealers during a three months' period in 1969. Of these it seems fair to single out for mention the one included in an article attributable to the editor of *Fichero,* Mary C. Turner, in the October 1968 issue. The choice of the monthly or bimonthly bulletin of the Librería Albe was due to the proprietor's having undertaken to add the name of the publisher to the bibliographical information provided, thereby making it possible for her to utilize the data for *Fichero.* One result is that the best single established source currently available for information as to the national bibliography of Uruguay is *Fichero.*

Comentarios bibliográficos americanos, a new, unorthodox, and interesting attempt to provide a cultural approach to information about the Spanish American book world, appeared in Montevideo in 1969. The initial issue was dated for the first quarter, but the editor, Eduardo Darino, indicated that the second issue was being published as a double, bimonthly number, after which the expectation was to publish the bibliography on a regular bimonthly basis. Since it quite naturally gives wider coverage of Uruguayan publications than does *Fichero,* it may well become the chief source of information concerning current Uruguayan publications, pending the time when an official agency can gain sufficient financial support to be able to carry out the bibliographic aspects of its responsibilities.

Summary

Uruguay experiences most of the difficulties common to its neighbors in attempting to produce a record of its national bibliography, but it has an advantage over many of them in the number and quality of the bibliographical services available. On the other hand, the country has some unique problems in that respect. Since the problems have so far outweighed the solutions, there is at present no effective national bibliography. The experience of Uruguay illustrates the possibility that recent developments in attempts to provide self-supporting, continent-wide bibliographies of current book production in the Spanish-speaking countries may offer a partial alternative to the traditional preparation of national bibliographies by national libraries on a non-self-supporting basis.

VENEZUELA

Venezuela has a sizable book production, but it lacks a strong bibliographic tradition. Although scholars had published important special bibliographies, the country owed the appearance of its first *Anuario bibliográfico venezolano* to a Spanish émigré, Pedro Grases. Under his able direction an *Anuario* covering materials published in Venezuela in 1942 and foreign ones about the country received in that year was published in 1944. Of the five additional volumes, the last covered 1947/1948. A later effort was made by Felipe Massiani and Carmen Luisa Escalante to update the *Anuario*. Two volumes covering the period 1949/1954 were published in 1960. The first listed books and pamphlets published in Venezuela. The second was devoted chiefly to foreign publications concerning Venezuela. It contained a comprehensive index to both volumes.

A *Boletín de la Biblioteca Nacional* has so far experienced three *épocas:* 1923-1933; 1936; 1959-1960.* It has contained some useful special bibliographies, but at least in its later periods it was not a source of information concerning the national bibliography.

In 1959 Venezuela, along with Argentina, contributed to the expansion of what had been for the three previous years the *Bibliografía de Centroamérica y del Caribe,* but which for that one year became the *Bibliografía de Centroamérica y del Caribe, Argentina y Venezuela.* The 1959 volume was to have been an intermediate step towards the publication of a comprehensive "Bibliografía de América Latina," an ambitious undertaking which did not materialize.

Meanwhile, for information about Venezuelan national bibliography the book world relied chiefly on information provided by periodicals. In a paper on "General Aspects of Bibliographic Activities in Venezuela" prepared for the Sixth Seminar (1961), Pedro Grases listed six reviews that he found helpful. Of these the most useful was the well-known *Revista nacional de cultura,* published by the Ministry of Education beginning in 1938. For many years it carried more or less regularly lists of "Obras ingresadas en la Biblioteca Nacional." At times these lists separated Vene-

* Suspended publication with *época* 3, No. 9, julio/septiembre 1960. Letter from Blanca Alvarez, Directora de la Biblioteca Nacional, June 30, 1969.

zuelan titles from those published elsewhere, but the arrangement was on a classified basis, without indexing. In 1965 the sponsorship was changed to the Instituto de Cultura y Bellas Artes. Its emphasis was shifted, and the bibliographic features were dropped.

During the early years of the 1960s the National Library was publishing its own record of publications received by it in what appears to have been a little known bulletin. The semiannual *Indice bibliográfico de la Biblioteca Nacional* was first published in 1956. It contained lists of library accessions arranged by (a) Venezuelan books or books relative to Venezuela and (b) foreign publications presented by country of origin. A single index of authors and anonymous works helped make the *Indice* a useful tool, but it became a retrospective one. Number 21, for July/December 1964 was the latest published until 1969. Numbers 22 and 23, covering 1965, were published in 1969 because the data had previously been assembled, but further issues were not planned.*

During the latter half of the decade the bibliographer and the would-be purchaser or research worker had to depend primarily on commercial sources for their information about Venezuelan books. However, for a country as advanced in many ways as Venezuela, its book industry has been exceptionally lacking in organization, and such catalogs as have been provided have often been deficient in basic information. The situation improved somewhat towards the end of the decade. It was a noteworthy event when one bookdealer, the Librería Politécnica, agreed to supply to *Fichero bibliográfico hispanoamericano* full data concerning as many Venezuelan publications as possible.† This cooperation was apparently responsible for the listing of five Venezuelan publishers in the April 1969 issue of *Fichero* as compared with one each in earlier issues for the year. *Comentarios bibliográficos americanos,* which began publication in Montevideo in 1969, also lists Venezuelan publishers as contributors.

Useful as *Fichero* and *Comentarios* may be for relatively current information, they are inadequate substitutes for a national bibliography, and it is good news that 1970 should see publication of the *Anuario bibliográfico venezolano* resumed, with excellent prospects for its being maintained on a current basis. In June 1969 there was named as the Director of the Biblioteca Nacional the first professional librarian to hold that office, Blanca Alvarez. Miss Alvarez holds a library science degree from one of the

* Letter from the Director of the National Library, dated August 7, 1969.

† Mary C. Turner, "Bibliografías corrientes de libros en nuestro idioma," *Fichero* 8:1 (Oct. 1968), pp. 6 f. Note on the catalog, *Libros nuevos venezolanos,* p. 8. Also, interview with Mrs. Turner, Editor of *Fichero,* May 2, 1969.

major universities in the United States and has had experience in various types of Venezuelan libraries.

Upon assuming office, Miss Alvarez gave high priority to resuming publication of the *Anuario*. In late June she stated* that the Biblioteca Nacional would try to publish an *Anuario* for 1967/1968 as soon as possible. It would then work on filling the gap since 1954 with a volume to cover 1954/1960 and another for 1961/1966. Clearly the state of the art in Venezuela is entering a new and promising phase.

Summary

The first *Anuario bibliográfico venezolano,* listing publications of 1942, was the work of a Spanish émigré, Pedro Grases. Later volumes covered only through 1954. In the absence of the other sources, great dependence has necessarily been placed on periodicals for information concerning Venezuelan publications. These have been supplemented recently by *Fichero* and *Comentarios bibliográficos americanos.* In June 1969 a professional librarian was appointed to head the National Library. She immediately gave high priority to the preparation of the *Anuario* for 1967/1968. Plans called for the filling of the gap from 1954 to 1966 as well as for the current publication of the *Anuario*.

* Letter, dated June 30, 1969. A letter dated August 7, 1969, stated that work on the 1967/1968 *Anuario* was well along and it should be ready for the printer soon.

III

THE INCLUSIVE CARIBBEAN AREA

THE CARIBBEAN AREA, in the broader sense, comprises a hetero-geneous group of republics and other political entities, with a correspond-ing variety of people and institutions. For present purposes the term "Caribbean area" includes not only the Greater and the Lesser Antilles but also Mexico, Central America, and Guyana.

The area, for all its diversity, has been the first in Latin America to develop regional bibliographies. *Current Caribbean Bibliography,* inaugu-rated in 1951 to provide a bibliographical record of publications in the dependent territories, has led a precarious existence, holds great possibili-ties, and is now at a critical stage. *The Bibliografía de Centroamérica y del Caribe,* an Havana-based and UNESCO-sponsored project designed to serve the island republics, the six Central American countries, and Puerto Rico, got off to a good start with a listing in 1958 of publications issued in 1956, but it foundered all too soon on difficulties such as finances, personnel changes due in large part to situations created by Castro, and to an overly ambitious expansion of the area for which coverage was attempted. Because the *BCAC* became, in the expanded 1959 volume, the *Bibliografía de Centroamérica y del Caribe, Argentina y Venezuela* and was to have become, beginning with the 1960 volume, the "Bibliografía de América Latina," its story was told in Chapter I. The *Bibliografía de*

Centroamérica y del Caribe remains a basic point of reference for Central America, and frequent reference will necessarily be made to it in discussing that area.

In Mexico only the Yucatán peninsula specifically belongs with the Caribbean area. Since the country is in fact a separate entity, it will be treated first.

MEXICO

Mexico is one of the chief publishing centers of Latin America, and it has a relatively strong bibliographical tradition. However, the records of its current national bibliography have, until recently, been relatively weak.

No full-length SALALM paper has been devoted to Mexican bibliography. The Second Seminar (1957) was concerned strictly with the acquisition of Mexican library materials. Papers dealt with that topic as such or the Mexican book industry and the status of exchanges in Mexico. (Possibly, at that early point, the relationship between bibliography and acquisitions was not yet established. At the next Seminar a paper included an appendix on "Bibliographical Sources Used in the Selection of Materials . . ." and the precedent was followed quite consistently later.) At the Fifth Seminar (1960) Mexico was one of a number of countries covered briefly by Fermín Peraza in his paper on "Bibliography in the Caribbean Area." About this time there were several contributions towards the Mexican national bibliography which were more or less attributable to interest generated by SALALM.

The Centro Mexicano de Escritores published in 1959 a 262-page *Catálogo de publicaciones periódicas mexicanas* which it had compiled "as a result of the need expressed at the Second Seminar." It listed some 450 titles published in the Federal District and another 250 or so in the states, plus additional lists for titles found recorded in the Hemeroteca (Serials Section) of the Biblioteca Nacional or elsewhere, but of which copies were not available for examination.

In 1961 Josefina Berroa, a Cuban librarian resident in Mexico, published *México bibliográfico, 1957-1960: catálogo general de libros impresos en México.* This list of 4,332 works, chiefly trade books, was primarily an author list, followed by a subject index. It was distributed in Mexico by the author and in the United States by R. R. Bowker, publisher of *Fichero bibliográfico hispanoamericano* and *Libros en venta.*

The *Boletín de la Biblioteca Nacional,* which had been published sporadically from 1904, began a new *época* in 1950. By 1960 it included a section, "Fichero," which consisted of the Library's quarterly list of recent acquisitions, chiefly Mexican imprints of various dates. In 1963 the title of the section was changed to "Bibliografía mexicana," but it remained a classified list with no author index and with no cumulation. Under the administration of Manuel Alcalá, beginning in 1958, the National Library improved its relationships with the Dirección General de Derecho de Autor, and a much larger portion of the country's production of books and pamphlets was listed than had previously been possible. It was quite true that the bibliographic section of the *Boletín* contains much useful information about Mexican publications, but it could scarcely be called a current national bibliography.

In the absence of other records the bimonthly *Boletín bibliográfico mexicano,* published regularly from 1940 by Porrúa Hermanos, became by default the chief source of information concerning current publishing in Mexico. It has contained various lists, such as "Nueva bibliografía mexicana" arranged alphabetically by author under an alphabetical list of subject headings, the firm's own list of its recent publications, and a list of books recently received from various sources "for its exclusive distribution." There is no cumulative feature, no author index is provided, and searching it for a particular item is a prohibitive task.

The factor of "exclusive distribution" is in fact a limiting one, since by the same sign no one Mexican dealer has access to all the publications appearing even in the Federal District. (The twenty-nine states have had very little coverage at any time.) The situation was improved somewhat with the appearance of *Fichero bibliográfico hispanoamericano,* since Mexico is one of the countries most extensively represented in the list of contributors to its monthly issues.

Within Mexico there has been no effective organization of dealers, such as the Sindicato Nacional do Livro in Brazil, an agency largely responsible for the *BBB: Boletim bibliográfico brasileiro,* which provided a useful supplement to the official bibliography during the 1950s and early 1960s, and the Cámara Argentina del Libro, which published *Biblos* from 1942 until the mid-1960s.

Still less has there been cooperation among dealers and librarians which might have led to the assembling of a more comprehensive bibliography than could be provided by any one publisher or dealer. Paul Bixler, a prominent college librarian whose recently published *The Mexican Library* is a report on a study made under Ford Foundation auspices, was struck by the lack of communication and cooperation he found among publishers, librarians, and educators. "Libraries and the publishing and distribution industries should be allies or at least friendly cooperators in the promotion of books and reading, but in Mexico they are not even friendly enemies; they do not speak to each other." Mr. Bixler was, as he indicates, much more familiar with library and publishing situations in Southeast Asia than in Latin America, but as a newcomer to the scene he was in a position to be objective. Similarities in some cases and differences in others served as bases for interesting and thought-provoking comparisons.

During the 1930s and the early 1940s an *Anuario bibliográfico mexicano* was published by various groups and individuals. The record is furnished by Arthur E. Gropp in his *Bibliography of Latin American Bibliographies* (1968). For a quarter of a century the title of *anuario* lay dormant, but in 1967 the Biblioteca Nacional, under the direction of Licenciado Ernesto de la Torre Villar, produced a 713-page *Anuario bibliográfico, 1958,* listing 4,289 titles published in that year. The date has already been noted as the point at which the effectiveness of the law of legal deposit had been greatly improved, largely through the efforts of the previous director, Manuel Alcalá. Selection of materials of the *Anuario* is based on the UNESCO specifications for statistics. Consequently, books and pamphlets (of 50 pages or less) published by government agencies and academic theses are included, as well as commercially produced publications, but serial publications of all types are excluded. Arrangement is on the decimal system pattern. In order to avoid cross references, an extensive "Indice analítico" (pp. 393-713) is provided, including subject references as well as a comprehensive name index. The preface stated that the *Anuario* was the first of a series and that the hope was to bring the *Anuario* up to date within a relatively short time. To the great credit of the Biblioteca Nacional, the expressed intentions are being realized. As of late August 1969 the Director stated that the volume for 1959 had been published and the 1960 volume was to be ready by early fall.*

Simultaneously with the appearance of the *Anuario bibliográfico,* which was to progress from the 1958 volume towards becoming a current annual publication, the Biblioteca Nacional and the Instituto Bibliográfico Mexicano started, as the current record, a bimonthly bulletin, *Bibliografía mexicana.* The foreword to the first issue, January/February 1967, stated the intention to include all significant books and pamphlets published in the Mexican Republic. The chief difficulty was seen as the chronic one of securing information from the various states, and assistance in that respect was requested in order that the Biblioteca Nacional and the Instituto

* Letter from the Director, Lic. Ernesto de la Torre Villar, dated August 30, 1969.

Bibliográfico Mexicano might comply with one of their basic objectives —to assemble the Mexican bibliographic production, to register it, and to diffuse the information.

The *Bibliografía mexicana* is to continue to appear in its six bimonthly issues, plus one or more supplements as needed, each with its own index. No cumulation is planned until such time as the *Anuario bibliográfico* shall have been produced through 1966. At that time, with the gap filled in, the *Anuario* will be updated from 1967 until it overtakes the bimonthly bulletin and can supersede it within a short time.

In addition to supplying this information, the Director stated that various other bibliographic projects were under way, such as bibliographic guides for humanities students at the University to accompany others already in progress in history, Mexican and Hispanic American literature, classics, pedagogy, and geography. Assistance had been given to other agencies to prepare Mexican bibliographies of philosophy and of jurisprudence. Additional bibliographies in preparation dealt with Mexican political parties and with writers of Jalisco, Chiapas, and San Luis Potosí, respectively. All this further explained why resources were not to be expended upon cumulating the *Bibliografía mexicana* as such.

Some confusion may arise from the fact that the *Anuario bibliográfico* and *Bibliografía mexicana* bear the imprint of the Biblioteca Nacional as publisher while "Universidad Nacional Autónoma de México" appears at the head of the title and also on the verso of the half-title page and title page respectively. In the latter case, below the name of the Rector (President) of the University and that of the Director of the National Library the words "Biblioteca Nacional e Instituto Bibliográfico Mexicano" are prominently displayed. The explanation is that late in the 1930s the National Library was made a division of the National Autonomous University of Mexico. The Instituto Bibliográfico Mexicano functions primarily as a technical institute within the university, so the relationships are interwoven. A discussion of the history and merits or disadvantages of the situation is beyond our province here, but some relevant questions are raised by Bixler in *The Mexican Library* (1969).

Official monographic publications appear frequently in the *Anuario* but less so in the bimonthly *Bibliografía mexicana,* an apparent discrepancy which may have a logical explanation. In any case, the 1940 compilation by Annita M. Ker, *Mexican Government Publications: a Guide to the More Important Publications of the National Government of Mexico, 1821-1936,* has recently been updated. *Las publicaciones oficiales de México: guía de publicaciones periódicas y seriadas, 1937-1967,* by Rosa

María Fernández Esquivel was called by the editors of the 1968 *Handbook of Latin American Studies* the most important work of its kind seen during the year. The guide was prepared as a thesis for a library science degree in the UNAM Facultad de Filosofía y Letras. Arrangement is by the legislative, executive, and judicial branches of government. Descriptive bibliographic information is provided as are also historical notes on the more important agencies. It is to be hoped that, now that a precedent has been established, a way will be found to keep the record more or less up to date.

Summary

Bibliographic developments in Mexico since the mid-1950s have been remarkable. The appearances in 1967 of a bimonthly bulletin, *Bibliografía mexicana,* and of an *Anuario bibliográfico, 1958,* first of a series which is working rapidly towards currency, are highly important developments. They remove Mexico from the ranks of the countries which are dependent chiefly upon the bulletins of bookdealers and other interested groups for information about the country's bibliographic output, and place it among the most advanced American countries in terms of the recording and publishing of its current national bibliography.

CENTRAL AMERICA

In any discussion involving the intellectual history of the Central American area, a few basic facts concerning its geography and history must be kept in mind. The six countries—Guatemala, Honduras, El Salvador, Nicaragua, Costa Rica, and Panama—occupy a narrow isthmus extending about 1,200 miles from Mexico to Colombia. The total area, some 220,000 square miles, is approximately that of California and New York combined. Mountains extending through most of the area affect climate, industries, and cultural life and have been an important factor in the shaping of historical events.

During the colonial period the area between Mexico and Panama constituted the Captaincy-General of Guatemala, under the Viceroyalty of New Spain, the seat of which was in Mexico City. For a few years, 1821-1838, the area became the United Provinces of Central America. Since that time the five republics have, generally speaking, gone their separate ways. In the 1960s there were evidences of a growing Central American consciousness, but not as yet in ways which have affected significantly the bibliographic record. Panama belongs with the group geographically and economically. Historically, it was included in the Viceroyalty of New Granada during the colonial period and was thereafter a part of Colombia until 1903, when it became independent.

The third centennial of the introduction of printing into Central America was celebrated by Guatemala in 1960. In contrast with the 1660 date of the earliest printing press in the former seat of the Captaincy-General of Guatemala, the first press in Honduras, its next-door neighbor, was set up in 1829. In Costa Rica the corresponding date was 1830.

Central American countries were considered individually in a paper on "Bibliography in the Caribbean Area" prepared by Fermín Peraza for the Fifth Seminar (1960). With respect to the Central American republics, it is particularly useful for its listing of the more important retrospective bibliographies, since there was little to be said otherwise beyond mention of the then current coverage by the *Bibliografía de Centroamérica y del Caribe*. Of the six countries, only Costa Rica could be credited with a truly current national bibliography.

The Seventh Seminar (1962) was devoted primarily to the consideration of Central America. Guatemala, Honduras, and Panama were represented by both working papers and participants. El Salvador and Nicaragua were not represented by either. In the absence of a paper or representative from Costa Rica, Carl Deal of the University of Kansas, which has Farmington Plan responsibility for Costa Rica, made some useful contributions. Representatives of Costa Rica and El Salvador presented papers later, at the Tenth Seminar.

The one Seventh Seminar paper which dealt with the entire area was that of Mrs. Edith Bayles Ricketson, Librarian of the Middle American Research Institute of Tulane University, whose topic was "The Acquisition of Research Materials from Central America and Panama and Their Selection." Her attempt to secure information by means of a questionnaire met with poor response. In reply to the question, "To what extent do you use non-national bibliographical data in your selection," the only positive answers scoring four or more were the following: Stechert-Hafner, 6; bookdealers' catalogs, 5; Pan American Union, *List of Books Accessioned,* 5; *Inter-American Review of Bibliography,* 4. Of national tools, the only one to score as high as four was, understandably, the *Anuario bibliográfico costarricense.*

Of the papers dealing with the countries of Central America, the one from Guatemala was the most informative. So much of it applies to other Central American countries that certain points may well be mentioned here. Gonzalo Dardón Córdova entitled his paper "Four Topics Concerning Books in Guatemala." The "Four Topics" as treated in their respective sections were: "The Book Industry in Guatemala," "Present Status of Exchange of Publications in Guatemala," "Extent to Which Guatemalan Publications Are Included in Bibliographies," and "Facilities Available in Guatemala for Photographic Reproduction." The same four topics were at least touched upon in the papers from Honduras and Panama, in compliance undoubtedly with specifications included with the invitation from SALALM to submit papers.

Since the only grist supplied to the bibliographer's mill consists of writing which has managed to get itself published in some form—whether as a mimeographed pamphlet, as a handsome letterpress volume, or in some intermediate form—it follows that the bibliographer is much concerned by the situation of the publishing industry in any country under discussion. (However, as Dardón Córdova pointed out, much of the most valuable material appears in periodicals and is therefore outside the range of the usual national bibliography.)

In summarizing his paper, Dardón Córdova made the following points: (1) in countries with a high illiteracy rate the vast majority of commercially published books are elementary texts; (2) the best publishers are the government and the national university; (3) few original works are published in editions as extensive as the 500 copies required for a book to be considered "commercially published"; (4) most of these works are in the humanities and the social sciences; and (5) there is need for technical works either in translation or as adaptations of parts or of the whole of useful materials, but much difficulty is encountered in securing the necessary permissions because of copyright restrictions.

In the paper itself and in the resulting discussion, a number of points applying to the region as a whole were brought out. Most of the participants had been aware that in Latin America small editions were the rule, but it was startling to learn that printings might be as diminutive as fifty copies. Of these, several or perhaps most would be for presentation to the author's friends. A few copies might be left on consignment in one or more bookstores. Once the author had settled his account, taking with him any unsold copies, the dealer might have no idea where to reach him, even if it occurred to him to do so. The normal reply to a request for the book, should one be made, would be *agotado*. Realistically, of course, in consideration of the effort involved, any commission received for the securing and, even more, for the mailing of a single copy would be very inadequate inducement.

It is for such reasons that the chief possibilities that the publications of the smaller and less developed countries may achieve such immortality as is afforded by bibliographical record lie in their being acquired by some more sophisticated method than has yet become customary. The regional bibliographical approach attempted by the *Bibliografía de Centroamérica y del Caribe* deserves credit as a "noble experiment." However, a basic weakness was that by the time information as to the existence of a given publication reached those who would be interested in securing it, the material was seldom to be had.

At present, chances seem dubious that the Central American countries, with the exception of Costa Rica, will soon develop effective means by which their own people and others can learn what national publications exist and can secure them if they wish to do so. As matters stand, the best immediate prospects for improving both the situation as to the acquiring of purchasable materials and of a corresponding bibliographic record's being made by some institution would seem to be further developments in those now existing, such as: (1) the Stechert-Hafner cooperative acquisitions plan, LACAP, (2) standing orders placed by libraries with local dealers equipped to handle them, where such dealers exist; (3) occasional visits by librarians or other institutional representatives. Resident national agents who might serve one or more institutions have been suggested, and perhaps the experiment has been tried. For publications which are not produced for sale, notably government documents and society publications, the exchange method will presumably continue to be the most effective one.

Assuming that the universities which have Farmington Plan responsibility for securing current publications of research value from a given area do acquire more materials from that area than does any other institution, it might be helpful for those libraries which are responsible for the various Central American republics to publish annual acquisitions lists. Such records would be of value to the countries themselves, which—again excepting Costa Rica—are apparently not now in a position to prepare and publish their own.

In the absence of lists from Farmington Plan libraries, there are two others which cover the area to a limited extent. Both, however, include publications of any date, as received by their respective libraries, thus restricting their value as "current bibliography."

The University of Florida Libraries have Farmington Plan responsibility only for the West Indies area, interpreted to include the Guianas and British Honduras (Belize), but University interests include the entire Caribbean region. This fact is reflected in the Libraries' acquisitions policies. Beginning in 1959 the Technical Processes Department of the University Libraries has published annual volumes entitled *Caribbean Acquisitions: Materials Acquired by the University of Florida.** At first the countries covered were those bordering on the Caribbean Sea and the Gulf of Mexico, but since 1964 Mexico has been excluded. As stated in the preface to the 1967 volume:

> *Caribbean Acquisitions* includes three different types of materials. First, it includes materials about the Caribbean published anywhere in the world. In this sense it serves as a selective subject bibliography. Secondly, it includes materials published in the Caribbean on any subject. In this sense it serves as a selective national bibliography. And finally, it includes works published by Caribbean authors who are living abroad.

Arrangement is by large topics: Art, Bibliography, Historical Sciences, Philosophy and Religion, Sciences and Technology, Social Science, and Other, with regional subdivisions under the principal subjects. An author index is provided. Beginning with the 1965/1966 volume, catalog cards have been reproduced, including Dewey Decimal numbers as assigned by the University of Florida Libraries.

The University of Texas Library, which began in the early sixties to publish national acquisitions lists, has more recently added regional ones where appropriate. In 1967 it published its first list of *Recent Acquisitions of Books, etc. from Central America by the Latin American Collection of the University of Texas Library*, covering 1962/1965. Arrangement is by country, with subject lists under some fifteen headings. There is no prefatory statement, nor is there an index. Catalog cards are reproduced, including Dewey Decimal numbers as assigned by the University of Texas Libraries. Assuming that later lists may be published at intervals of from two to four years, as has been the case with others of the Texas lists, they qualify as "current" only as compared with the occasional *anuarios* or other bibliographical records published at long and irregular intervals, if at all, by most of the countries themselves.

As elsewhere in Latin America, when national tools are lacking the

---

* Exceptions to the "annual" term have been the first volume, covering 1957/58, and one for 1965/66. Materials catalogued by the Law, Agriculture, and Health Center Libraries are not included.

most apparent avenues for making known the existence of newly published materials are (1) through the pages of the two commercially sponsored bibliographies, *Fichero bibliográfico hispanoamericano* (1961-) and
the recently inaugurated *Comentarios bibliográficos americanos* (1969-)
and (2) through dealers' catalogs—primarily, for Central America, the
Stechert-Hafner LACAP lists.

It is to be hoped that national authors and printers will increasingly avail
themselves of these services and that they will endeavor to make the
publications listed available to potential purchasers for a longer period of
time than is now the case. As a result of increased sales, editions could be
larger, dealers' profits would increase, and even the author himself might
receive at least token remuneration. Also, some of the manuscripts now
unpublished because of lack of means or of inducement might emerge
from limbo and become a part of the national patrimony of the country in
question.

An additional source of information about Central American publications should be mentioned here, although for present purposes bibliographies appearing in periodicals are generally excluded. An important
feature of *Caribbean Studies,* the quarterly journal of the Institute of
Caribbean Studies of the University of Puerto Rico, is the extensive
section "Current Bibliography." Primary emphasis is upon the Antilles,
but the Caribbean area in general and the various Central American
countries (as part of the "Circum Caribbean") receive attention in more or
less alternate issues. Coverage for periodical articles is superior to that for
books and pamphlets. Of the latter group, a considerable portion are
government documents, but a significant number of monographs are
included, both commercial and noncommercial publications.

COSTA RICA

Costa Rica is the one Central American country which really has a current
national bibliography. Its record is in fact one of the best among those of
the Latin American republics.

The lack of a working paper devoted to Costa Rica at the Seventh
Seminar (1962) was remedied at the Tenth (1965), when Srta. Nelly
Kopper (Assistant Director of the University of Costa Rica Library), as the
General Secretary of the Asociación Costarricense de Bibliotecarios, pre-
sented an excellent one. Miss Kopper was listed as the *compiladora
nacional* for Costa Rica in the first volume (1956) of the *Bibliografía de*

Centroamérica y del Caribe. Later volumes, 1957-1959, credited the group, the Asociación Costarricense de Bibliotecarios, with serving in that capacity.

For a number of years previously, a *Boletín bibliográfico,* published by the Biblioteca Nacional, had provided an alphabetical author list of Costa Rican publications. It was superseded in 1956 by the *Anuario bibliográfico costarricense,* a subject list, based on a long, alphabetical list of subject headings, with an author index provided. The data were the same as those provided to the *BCAC,* but publication in the *Anuario* retained national identity, which was largely lost in the subject approach employed by the *BCAC.*

The *Anuario* was compiled, according to the foreword, by the Comité Nacional de Bibliografía Adolfo Blen, a committee of the Asociación Costarricense de Bibliotecarios. Acknowledgment to several institutions, such as the Ministerio de Educación Pública, the Biblioteca Nacional, the Biblioteca de la Universidad de Costa Rica, Biblioteca del Banco Central, and the Imprenta Nacional, as well as to individuals who had collaborated in the preparation of the *Anuario,* intimated something as to the scope of the Comité Nacional in whose name the bibliography was published.

The *Anuario* has continued to appear regularly and promptly, published by the Ministerio de Educación Pública. The address given is that of the Asociación, but it had seemed possible that there had survived in Costa Rica one of the national bibliographic committees set up in the mid-1950s under UNESCO auspices. However, in reply to a question concerning the situation, Miss Kopper stated that although the group designation continues, she has been entirely responsible for the compilation for the past four years.* In the same letter in which she acknowledged her present full responsibility for the *Anuario,* Miss Kopper paid tribute to Fermín Peraza, the Director Técnico de la Bibliografía de Centroamérica y del Caribe, saying that he and his wife, Elena, had taught her what she knew of library science in the courses they offered in Panama a number of years ago. This illustrates how much the personal factor enters into the nature of bibliographical developments in Latin America.

In her SALALM paper (1965) "The Booktrade in Costa Rica; the Present State of Costa Rican Bibliography ..." Miss Kopper supplied a bibliography of Costa Rican bibliographies. Of the most famous, the *Indice bibliográfico de Costa Rica* by Luis Dobles Segreda, she listed the nine volumes published and stated that two additional volumes—volume 10, on Education (1843-1935) and Sociology and Demography

* Letter to this writer, dated October 3, 1969.

(1843-1932), and volume 11, Poetry (1851-1930)—were in press. In her recent communication she stated that they were published in 1967, and noted that the editing had been done by the Asociación Costarricense de Bibliotecarios. The Dobles Segreda work is prepared, as indicated by the nature of the two new volumes, as a subject approach.

The *Anuario* includes official publications on a subject basis, but the index, arranged by author, individual or corporate, provides references to publications of the various agencies. Periodicals are not included. A *Lista de tesis de grado de la Universidad de Costa Rica* has been published annually since 1957, according to Miss Kopper's SALALM paper. It is arranged by colleges but is indexed by author and subject.

The limited amount of publishing done in Costa Rica, one of the more literate Latin American countries, is accounted for by Miss Kopper in a brief but excellent statement. A small market, rising costs of labor and of materials, and taxes on paper and on machinery and equipment were blamed. She noted that many editions consisted of a few mimeographed copies. She placed the production of books and pamphlets in 1963 at 220. A list of four firms which would export books was given.

At the Seventh Seminar (1962) Carl W. Deal, representing the University of Kansas (which has Farmington Plan responsibility for the acquisition of materials from Costa Rica) commented that Antonio Lehmann, proprietor of the Librería Lehmann, could be depended upon to supply commercial publications. The chief difficulty lay in the securing of government documents and those of semi-autonomous agencies, for which no adequate listing was found. There are also several important international agencies with headquarters in Costa Rica for which no regular listing or source of procurement exists.

Summary

The number and nature of Costa Rican publications are limited by the high costs involved. However, the country has provided a continuous record of its publications since 1946. It is the one country which still maintains the system it established in 1956 for providing information to the now defunct *Bibliografía de Centroamérica y del Caribe*.

EL SALVADOR

El Salvador, like Costa Rica, was not represented at the Seventh Seminar but did submit a paper for the Tenth (1965). "Book Publishing in El

Salvador," by the General Direction of Libraries and Archives of El Salvador, includes a long list of publishers and printers, not only in San Salvador but in other municipalities as well, and a correspondingly long list of bookstores. Together they would indicate that there is a considerable bibliographic output in this smallest, but most densely populated, of the Spanish American republics.

The section on "Bibliography" consists of half a page of text followed by "Works Which List the Titles of Publications." An *Anuario bibliográfico salvadoreño* was listed only for 1952. Authorship was attributed to the Biblioteca Nacional. It was described as including books published in El Salvador, books by Salvadorean authors published elsewhere, and books which refer to El Salvador.

A paragraph in the introductory section of this Tenth Seminar paper stated that the National Library was reorganizing its catalogs. It was taking advantage of the situation to begin "the work necessary for the Salvadorean bibliographical annual." At the same time it was working towards the preparation of various tools for the use of persons interested in the retrospective bibliography of the country.

Bibliography, Documentation, and Terminology for September 1968 contained a section on El Salvador, but the data were for 1966. As "National Bibliography" it listed, without identification, *Bibliografía salvadoreña, Bibliografía de publicaciones oficiales,* and a *Bibliografía cronológica salvadoreña.* Of these, none was included in the 1965 SALALM paper except the first, which is presumably a *Lista preliminar de la biblioteca salvadoreña,* a 430-page mimeographed list prepared by the Biblioteca Nacional in 1952.

El Salvador is a country in which the government has had an extensive and long-maintained program for the publishing of literary works by its Ministry of Culture. During the years covered by the *Bibliografía de Centroamérica y del Caribe* (1956-1959), when Baudilio Torres, Director of the National Library, was the National Compiler, they were included in the *BCAC.* Since 1956, inasmuch as the works have been distributed rather widely to the national libraries of other countries and to institutions which maintain exchange arrangements with the ministry, they do appear in the bibliographies prepared by foreign recipients.

Since the publications of the Ministry of Culture include so large a portion of important Salvadorean contemporary writing and of reprints of earlier works, the record as presented in *Guión literario,* the monthly bulletin published from 1956 by the Editorial Department of the Ministry of Culture, which includes a section listing its publications, does provide a significant, though partial, record of the national bibliography. The *Guión literario* is the only item listed by Fermín Peraza for El Salvador in the 1969 edition of his *Bibliografías corrientes de la América Latina.* At present it runs considerably behind date but is still being distributed (1967 issues in 1969).

Summary

El Salvador appears to have published no *Anuario bibliográfico* since 1952. The only dependable bibliographic tool is the *Guión literario* (1956-), prepared and distributed by the Ministry of Culture, which itself maintains an extraordinary program of publishing and distributing important national works.

GUATEMALA

Various sources, including the Fermín Peraza *Bibliografías corrientes de la América Latina* (1969), list the *Anuario bibliográfico guatemalteco,* 1960- and the *Indice bibliográfico guatemalteco,* 1951- as "current," presumably because of their open entries and the lack of any specific information that they have suspended publication. However, it seems that only the one issue of the *Anuario* has been recorded, and the latest issue of the *Indice* is that for 1959/1960.

The *Anuario bibliográfico guatemalteco* for 1960 was apparently distributed to some extent as a separate work, but the copy at hand constitutes pages 137-67 of an issue of the *Revista de la Biblioteca Nacional* which appeared in 1962 (época 4, año 1, 1962) and which seems to have been the only issue to date of the fourth *época.* This corresponds with the entry in "A Selective List of Latin American Bibliographies Appearing in 1962," as presented by Jorge Grossmann to the Eighth Seminar (1963). However, Arthur E. Gropp in his *Bibliography of Latin American Bibliographies* (1968) gives it a separate entry as a publication of the Biblioteca Nacional. Gonzalo Dardón Córdova in his above cited contribution to the Seventh Seminar (1962), "Four Topics Concerning Books in Guatemala," also listed the *Anuario* separately, noting that it was prepared in "Homenaje de la Biblioteca Nacional de Guatemala en el CXL aniversario de nuestra independencia nacional" and that the compilation was by Enrique Polonsky Célcer (Guatemala, 1961).

Of the *Indice bibliográfico guatemalteco,* 1951- , Gropp (1968) says: "1951-1952 published by the Servicio Extensivo of the Biblioteca Nacional, and 1958 by the Instituto Guatemalteco-Americano. Publication suspended 1953-1957. Last issue received at PAU: 1959-1960."

What these facts do not indicate is that the compiler in both cases was Dardón Córdova. In his Seventh Seminar paper he included in a list of works· in progress the *Indice bibliográfico* for 1961-1962. However, it appears not to have achieved publication. In the *Indice*, which combined an author and subject approach, Dardón Córdova listed only works which he himself had handled, and he attempted to bring it out as promptly as possible. A large portion of the items indexed were articles which had appeared in periodicals or newspapers.

In Latin America the state of the national bibliography is often largely dependent upon individual efforts, such as those of Gonzalo Dardón Córdova. He studied library science at the University of Michigan in 1945-1946 under a grant from the United States Office of Education. Upon his return to Guatemala, he became active in promoting international cooperation. He has compiled various special bibliographies in order to make the work of national authors better known at home and elsewhere. According to information reaching this writer, Dardón Córdova left the Instituto Guatemalteco-Americano to return to the Biblioteca Nacional to teach in the Library School conducted by it. This would account for the lack of later issues of the *Indice guatemalteco* than the one for 1959/1960.

With respect to its official publications Guatemala does provide a partial record which is unique in Latin America. Its Tipografía Nacional, which was established in 1892, observed a half-century of service by publishing in 1944 a *Catálogo general de libros, folletos, y revistas editados en la Tipografía Nacional de Guatemala desde 1892 hasta 1943.* The precedent has been followed by later volumes, one covering 1944-1953 and another for 1954-1962, published in 1954 and 1963 respectively. We may therefore hope that this important record will continue to be updated at ten year intervals.

Inasmuch as the government is the chief publisher of the country, this list is a valuable as well as an intriguing one. It lists in chronological order of publication *memorias* of various ministries, decrees, presidential speeches, and some less obviously official documents, such as books presumably intended as history or other texts, and even such items as a program for a concert sponsored by El Comité de Damas Leones de Guatemala and given by a Chilean pianist (October 1961). Periodicals listed range from apparently local bulletins to the important *Anales de la Sociedad de Geografía e Historia de Guatemala* (1924-). Bibliographic information provided by the *Catálogo* is complete, including the number of copies printed of a given item. However, in Guatemala, as elsewhere, not all agencies issue their publications through their government printing office. The ability of the Tipografía to print nondocumentary items is undoubtedly determined by financial and other limitations. During the latest decade reported, the number of items printed per month seldom was as high as ten, and for some months a single item was listed. In spite of its limitations, the *Catálogo* does provide in its successive volumes a continuing record of an important part of the national bibliography.

Guatemala may be at present a laggard in its production of "current" national bibliography, but it stands unrivaled in the Americas for having achieved a published record of its retrospective bibliography, down to a comparatively recent date. In January 1960 the Consejo de Ministros, with presidential consent, declared "el año del Tricentenario de la Imprenta en Centro América" and commissioned the Ministerio de Gobernación to set up a suitable Central American program. A month later the designated ministry named a Central Committee in Guatemala and recommended that similar committees be formed elsewhere in Central America. Apparently the latter recommendation had no significant outcome, but in Guatemala the result was a monumental series of ten volumes, which constitute the Colección Bibliográfica del Tercer Centenario de la Fundación de la Primera Imprenta en Centro América. The entire record of the project is given in the final volume, which also provides in the preface a valuable historical outline of Guatemalan bibliography. The preface is signed by David Vela, Chairman of the Executive Committee, whose members were elected from among those of the Central Committee.

The final volume of the series, *Bibliografía guatemalteca, años 1951-1960 (Una década),* was compiled by Gilberto Valenzuela Reyna (as were also volumes 6 to 9, covering the years 1861-1950). It was published by the Tipografía Nacional in 1964. The Executive Committee, having thus fulfilled its mission of providing a record of Guatemalan publishing from 1660 to 1960, was dissolved. The series is, therefore, definitely concluded. However, it has helped, among other things, to establish for Guatemala a strong bibliographic tradition.

Bibliografía guatemalteca, 1951-1960, lists 1,070 numbered items. Arrangement is chronological by year, with entries alphabetical by author for each year. Not only are full bibliographic data provided, but so also are descriptive annotations which add immeasurably to the value of the work. Official publications and university theses are included. In extraordinary cases presidential decrees or congressional resolutions are given in full.

Individual issues of periodicals are noted, sometimes with contents notes. An author index is provided.

Summary

The record of publishing in Guatemala is important not only for itself but for what it represents for the rest of Central America. This fact was illustrated recently by Guatemala's publication of the ten-volume *Bibliografía guatemalteca* covering the three centuries, 1660-1960.

Neither the *Anuario bibliográfico guatemalteco* nor the *Indice bibliográfico guatemalteco* has appeared since 1960, but their compilers and others have demonstrated that the necessary skills for the preparation of a creditable national bibliography exist, and it is to be hoped that the resources for the resumption of its publication can be made available soon.

In any case, it seems a reasonable assumption that the Tipografía Nacional may be expected to follow its own precedent and will publish for the decade 1963-1972 its own important part of the record.

HONDURAS

For the Seventh Seminar (1962), which concentrated on Central America, a paper was submitted on "The Booktrade, Bibliography, and Exchange of Publications in Honduras" with an annex, "Recent Official Publications of the Government of Honduras." The authors were Ernesto Alvarado García, Julio Armando Ponce, and Ernesto Alvarado Reina.

The government has been and is the country's chief publisher, both under its own imprint and that of the Imprenta Aristón. Letterpress printing shops now exist and do good work, but the few books they produce are (as elsewhere under similar circumstances) in small editions and expensive. Authors are still expected to give their books away free. The same point, but with a suggestion as to means of improving the situation, had been made by Licenciado Jorge Fidel Durón, who was quoted as follows: "Even though it is still the exception to sell a book, since we cling to the custom of giving and expecting to be given books by national authors, it would still be possible to seek, through book fairs and literary exhibitions, to inform the great reading public about authors who are making an attempt to have their works published."

In the section on the exchange of publications, the authors of the SALALM paper stated that for economic reasons the international exchange of publications had declined, although official agencies still maintained exchange service with other countries. However, the postal authorities were not currently allowing the "Pan American postal exemption on publications, letters, and postcards addressed to foreign countries for the purpose of international relations and exchange." Therefore, all offices "have to pay the required postage, which constitutes a further serious obstacle to the exchange of publications." Action by the Pan American Union was solicited. It was noted that some Honduran authors sent copies of their works to libraries in other countries.

The exchange situation illustrates the fact that a lack of a national bibliography may be compensated for to some extent if a country's publications are widely distributed elsewhere, so that a record is provided (for instance, by *Caribbean Acquisitions* of the University of Florida Libraries, and eventually, by the Library of Congress's *Subject Catalog: Books*) from which information can later be retrieved by national bibliographers.

The one-page account of "The Inclusion of National Works in Bibliographies" in the Seventh Seminar paper began: "The pioneer of national bibliography in Honduras was Prof. Rafael Heliodoro Valle, who was followed by Jorge Fidel Durón. . . ." Rafael Heliodoro Valle (1891-1959) was an important bibliographer not only of Honduras but of Central America, and to a lesser extent of Latin America. The list of references under his name in the *Author Index to the Handbook of Latin American Studies, Nos. 1-28, 1936-1966* (1968) is perhaps the longest found there. He was a frequent contributor of bibliographic notes, including occasional ones on current publications, to *Honduras rotaria* (1943-) the remarkable Honduran organ of International Rotary, which has recently celebrated its twenty-fifth anniversary. Celebration of the *Honduras rotaria* anniversary properly included homage to its editor, Jorge Fidel Durón. As a devotee of the international principles of the organization, he has done much to subsidize this most important general periodical published in Honduras through a great expenditure of time (and quite possibly of his own funds) in order that it may the better serve its purpose at home and elsewhere.

The relevant point here is that Sr. Durón comprehends the needs both for a people to know its heritage of the written word and for that record to be available to others. Consequently, in the same year *Honduras rotaria* was founded, he assembled and published the *Repertorio bibliográfico hondureño,* calling it "the first tentative and rudimentary attempt in Honduras to create a national bibliography." In 1946 the Imprenta Calderón published his revised and enlarged work, *Indice de la bibliografía hondureña.* The prefaces indicate that both works were compiled as a service, in the absence of other records, and that he hoped the task would be better performed by others.*

However, lacking a substitute, Sr. Durón continued to do what he could in the interests of national bibliography. He served as the Honduran *compilador nacional* for the *Bibliografía de Centroamérica y del Caribe* during the first three years of its existence, 1956-1958. (In the final volume, 1959, Honduras was not listed as being among the countries represented.) He also contributed from time to time comments on either individual Honduran writers and their works or notes concerning publications of a given year. In an article "Los Libros y publicaciones de 1960," in *Honduras rotaria* for May/June 1961, Durón not only provided the information indicated but stated that his *Indice de la bibliografía hondureño* had been brought up to date as of 1957 but that his duties as a government official had prevented his editing and publishing the new edition.

After a lapse of several years (since 1961?) Sr. Durón published in *Honduras rotaria* for February/April 1968 a bibliographic essay on "Libros y publicaciones de 1967" which provided a very useful descriptive account of monographs (number of pages not stated), government publications, and periodicals published during the year. In the concluding paragraph he wrote eloquently of the importance of the record of national writings for the social and cultural history of the country and emphasized the need for a complete imprint for both books and periodicals, indicating by whom and when they were published. He concluded by restating his hope that soon, in the national interest, someone with more ability and resources than he possessed would develop this intangible wealth.

It appeared early in the 1960s that the more sophisticated record which Durón has urgently advocated was to become a reality. In their 1962 SALALM paper, the authors stated flatly: "No bibliographical yearbook has been published by any official or private body." No mention was made of a work in progress, but a year later, in June 1963, there appeared the first such record. The *Anuario bibliográfico hondureño* for 1961, published by the Editorial del Ministerio de Educación Pública in 1963, was prepared by the Director of the National Library, Miguel Angel García. It is a 49-page printed pamphlet which presents an extensive listing of books, pamphlets, mimeographed reports—well organized and with complete bibliographic data—followed by an 8-page list of newspapers and newssheets and a 3-page list of "Revistas" and of "Boletines." For none of these periodicals, however, are dates or addresses given. Arrangement of the monographs is by

* For further description and comment, see Zimmerman, *Guide to Current Latin American Periodicals* (1961), p. 128.

subject, the ten groups being those of the decimal system. In the foreword Professor García urged managers and proprietors of printing establishments to provide full bibliographic data, including in particular the year, and to send copies of their publications for future *Anuarios.*

That the publication of this *Anuario* was a landmark in Honduran bibliography is attested by an interesting article, "Bibliografía retrospectiva," by "Microbius Bibliothecarius" in *Honduras rotaria* for January/ March 1969. In Part I, written originally in 1964, the author stated that the period to be covered as retrospective bibliography would be from 1830 when the first printing press was set up in Honduras through 1960, since the *Anuario bibliográfico hondureño* began publication in 1961.

That the *Anuario* was first published in 1963 with a listing of publications for 1961 is an established fact. What later issues were prepared and distributed is less clear. Abel Rodolfo Geoghegan, in his *Obras de referencia de América Latina* (1965), says that the 1962 issue of the *Anuario* appeared late in 1963 in typewritten form. It seems that a cumulated issue for 1961/1963 was distributed also, perhaps on a limited basis. The 1968 volume of the *Handbook of Latin American Studies* lists an issue for 1961/1963 and says about it: "National bibliography for the period cited. . . ."

Whatever the record, it is certain that an important precedent has been established by the Biblioteca Nacional. Besides providing a record for a limited period, it demonstrated that the essential bibliographic skills do (or did) exist in Honduras, and it strongly advocated to publishers that they supply the needed data.

Summary

Honduras has no established current national bibliography, but it has an intriguing bibliographic record. Two eminent Hondurans, Rafael Heliodoro Valle (1891-1959) and Jorge Fidel Durón (1902-) made the chief contributions up until 1960. Durón continues to provide occasional important bibliographical essays on current national publications through the medium of *Honduras rotaria.* In 1963 the Biblioteca Nacional published an *Anuario bibliográfico* for 1961, thereby establishing an important precedent.

NICARAGUA

Nicaragua is the only one of the Latin American republics which did not provide the Seminars with some account of its publications and bibliographic activities by 1965, date of the Tenth Seminar. By that time the Seminars had attempted to cover all of Latin America and the Caribbean area.

Until now the only systematic record of Nicaraguan publications is contained in the three small volumes of the *Bibliografía de trabajos publicados en Nicaragua* which were compiled by the American Library of Nicaragua for the years 1943, 1944, and 1945-1947 and published as numbers 1, 6, and 7-9 of its bibliographic series.*

When the *Bibliografía de Centroamérica y del Caribe* (1956-1959) was inaugurated, it was expected that it would be able to include Nicaraguan publications on the same basis as was done for other countries. However, for the first three years, lacking a national compiler, Marietta Daniels provided such information as was available from the files of the Pan American Union Library. In 1959 Fidel Colombo González was listed as the *compilador nacional.* A section on Nicaragua in the UNESCO bulletin *Bibliography, Documentation, and Terminology* for March 1969 listed as "National Bibliography" only the following:

Universidad Nacional de Nicaragua. Biblioteca Nacional. *Lista de tesis de la Facultad de Ciencias Jurídicas y Sociales que hay en la Biblioteca Central.* 1941-1965. Vol. 1: in chronological order (published in 1966). Vol. II: in alphabetical order, according to subject (in preparation).

Under these circumstances it appears that the "best" source for information concerning Nicaraguan publications is the one ranked highest by the returns to the questionnaire circulated by Edith Ricketson for the Seventh Seminar (1962), the Stechert-Hafner LACAP lists. When and if these lists begin to supply the necessary bibliographical data, including publisher, to qualify the items for listing in the *Fichero bibliográfico hispanoamericano,* at least the cumulated record should become available. What information will be supplied by the new *Comentarios bibliográficos americanos,* which began publication in Montevideo in 1969, remains to be seen. Otherwise, information will continue to be limited chiefly to data provided by the records of acquired items catalogued by institutions which secure significant numbers of publications from Nicaragua.

Summary

Nicaragua has given scant evidence until now of interest in establishing and maintaining a record of the few publications issued in the country or of

* The extraordinary story behind their compilation, as related in the introductions to the first two numbers, is summarized in Zimmerman, *Guide to Current Latin American Periodicals* (1961), p. 163.

having developed competent national bibliographers who might compile such a record.

PANAMA

Panama was represented in person at the Seventh Seminar (1962) by Sra. Carmen D. de Herrera and by a 14-page paper prepared by her and by others and entitled "The Booktrade, Bibliography, and Exchange of Publications in Panama." In her section on "The Book Industry in Panama," Sra. Herrera mentioned several publishers well equipped but faced with such difficulties as a shortage of professional personnel, the high cost of paper, and a lack of capital. She listed four factors which had impeded the development of the book industry in Panama:

1. Because of a lack of stimulus, writers are few, and unpublished works are many.
2. Publishing costs are very high, and many authors resort to foreign publishing houses where their books can be published more commercially.
3. The very limited editions are soon exhausted.
4. The high cost of books limits the market and thus it is not possible to distribute Panamanian books inside and outside the country as would be desirable.

Among the conclusions she draws from these facts is "that the lack of books, especially textbooks, leads us to use foreign texts in teaching, thus affecting the national economy and education."

At the same Seminar the Guatemalan representative, Sr. Gonzalo Dardón Córdova, complained about copyright restrictions on the translation of textbooks, but Panama is the only Central American country which, so far as is recorded in SALALM papers, has noted that many of its authors have their writings published outside the country. Special characteristics of the Panamanian situation, both historical and geographical, explain this additional limitation upon the data available within the country as material for a national bibliography.

Enrique A. Noriega was responsible for a one-page section, "The Inclusion of National Works in Bibliographies." He cited a 1946 law which had provided that the National Library should be the repository for published works and that the national bibliography should be maintained. In 1955 a National Bibliographic Center had been founded, "composed of a group of librarians, educators and historians." The *compiladora nacional,* Carmen D. de Herrera, had been providing the requisite data to the *Bibliografía de Centroamérica y del Caribe* for each year through 1960, and for 1961 in what was to have become the "Bibliografía de América Latina."

Sr. Noriega wrote of the efforts of the Panamanian Association of Librarians and of resolutions made in connection with the Second Bibliographic Seminar, directed towards securing compliance with the law of legal deposit and for the compilation of the national bibliography. Two working groups had been formed to compile the bibliography, "one in the National Library charged with the bibliography on periodical publications and the other in the Library of the University to work up the bibliography of books and pamphlets."

The Seminar to which Sr. Noriega referred was the Segundo Seminario Bibliográfico de Centro América y del Caribe, held at the National University of Panama on February 24-28, 1958. This writer gladly testifies to the extraordinary efforts of the Grupo Bibliográfico (which had been formed in 1955 under UNESCO auspices) not only to provide suitable conditions for a successful seminar but to make important contributions to the national bibliography through special compilations, most of which were unfortunately not otherwise published. It was in accordance with the working arrangements of the Bibliographic Group that the National Compiler, who was responsible for sending to the Technical Director of the *BCAC* the entries for Panama, should be the Director of the Library of the National University.

Some attempt was made to continue the record of the national bibliography after the demise of the *BCAC.* Fermín Peraza's *Bibliografías corrientes de la América Latina* (1969) carries this entry:

Panama (ciudad) Universidad. Grupo Bibliográfico. *Bibliografía de libros y folletos, 1958-1960,* por la Lic. Carmen D. de Herrera. Panamá, 1960. 44 h.

However, the sixties were a troubled decade in Panama. Its troubles involved the closing down at intervals of the National University, thereby making it impossible for its Librarian, Sra. Herrera, to continue to carry out the bibliographic responsibilities originally assigned to her by the Grupo Bibliográfico.

As it is, credit must be given to the small country which profited so greatly from two summer sessions of library science offered in 1949 and 1950 by Fermín Peraza, Marietta Daniels, and others that in 1958 it could organize a bibliographic group and could produce the bibliographies prepared for the Segundo Seminario Bibliográfico. It can be hoped that files are being maintained, and that in better days Panama can prepare and publish regularly the record of its national publications.

Meanwhile, as in similar cases, we are dependent for current Panamanian information largely upon (1) the "Current Bibliography" section in *Caribbean Studies* and (2) the broader coverage in *Fichero bibliográfico hispanoamericano, Comentarios bibliográficos americanos,* and LACAP catalogs. For cumulative data we must depend upon such sources as the bibliographic publications made available by institutions which systematically acquire materials from the area and publish annually or at other intervals the records of the items catalogued.

Summary

Panama has no current national bibliographic record, nor has an *anuario* been published. However, it does have competent bibliographers who have made individual contributions through other means, and it seems a reasonable assumption that both the National Library and the library of the National University of Panama are doing all that circumstances permit to maintain current records of Panamanian monographs and serials. Meanwhile, for both current and cumulated information we must rely entirely upon secondary sources.

THE WEST INDIES

In terms of current "Latin American" bibliography, as it is generally thought of, consideration of the West Indies would be limited to the three "Latin" republics and to Puerto Rico. For three of these, the paper by Fermín Peraza on "Bibliography in the Caribbean Area," submitted to the Fifth Seminar (1960), concluded after some discussion of bibliographic backgrounds that the *Bibliografía de Centroamérica y del Caribe (1956-1959)* was the principal tool. The exception was Cuba, whose *Anuario bibliográfico cubano* he was still editing from his home base at the Municipal Library in Havana.

The 1960s proved to be a decade of ferment. A significant portion of the yeast came from the Caribbean area—most notably, of course, from Fidel Castro's Cuba. But other events were also taking place, and movements were in process that were changing political, economic, cultural, and social facts and relationships. New countries were emerging. The character of the Organization of American States was beginning to be modified by the admission of the first English-speaking countries other than the United States of America.

Such circumstances affect bibliographic records directly and indirectly. Lines of regional development during the last quarter of a century, and particularly in the past decade, were toward cooperation among the English-speaking dependencies and Puerto Rico. The latter, if only theoretically bilingual, is sufficiently so among persons equipped to function in responsible library positions that it alone has participated in both the experience of the *Bibliografía de Centroamérica y del Caribe* and that of the "dependencies" group which *Current Caribbean Bibliography* (1951-) was primarily designed to serve.

The circumstances which made the *BCAC* experiment possible belong to a bygone era, as do also those which brought the *CCB* into being. However, the fortunes of the latter have been closely related to the evolution of new economic and political patterns in the area. *Current Caribbean Bibliography* was designed as a tool to promote regional development. The fact that it survives and is part of a situation which has brought modern-age bibliographic services for the area to the threshold of realization is no accident. Too great credit cannot be given to the British tradition and practice of providing its colonial areas with public servants equipped with career training. For their part, Puerto Rico and the Virgin Islands have shared fully in the possibilities for self-improvement offered by the "G.I. Bill of Rights," the National Defense Education Act, and the Library Services Acts. It is to their credit that they have taken full advantage of the proffered opportunities.

The three "Latin republics," meanwhile, have gone their separate ways. Of the three, only Cuba has an established basis for library and bibliographic services, and unfortunately its present situation precludes full participation in bibliographic or other regional enterprises. The Dominican Republic and Haiti have only recently begun to evince any interest in the possibilities of cooperative bibliographic developments.

In the interests of continuity, it seems best to consider areas in the following order: (1) "The Caribbean" as an emerging entity, (2) Puerto Rico, (3) Cuba, (4) the Dominican Republic, (5) Haiti, and (6) the English-speaking West Indies.

"THE CARIBBEAN"—AN EMERGING ENTITY

As a bibliographic point of reference, the Fifth Seminar, held at the New York Public Library June 14-16, 1960, is basic. It was seminal in several respects, but for present purposes the third session, on "Consideration of Problems of Acquisition from the Caribbean Islands," was fundamental, and the fourth, on "Considerations of the Problems Relating to the Exchange of Publications in the Americas," with particular emphasis on the Caribbean area, was also important. The reports of the discussions based on the papers presented, as recorded in the *Final Report and Working Papers* published by the Pan American Union in 1965, serve as reminders that in the midst of past and present ferment there are some constant factors which need to be kept in mind.

One of the most basic of the constant factors is the great diversity that exists in the Caribbean in the physical makeup and resources of the islands themselves and also of their inhabitants. Events since 1940 and the advent of the air age have begun to change things, but communications among the islands are still minimal, while interests and loyalties are predominantly, if not exclusively, those of the individual islands. Ties with the present or former "metropolitan powers" of which the islands are or have been dependencies have tended to wane or even to be severed.

It took the hard realities of the Second World War to bring the several sovereign powers with dependencies in the Caribbean to take the first measures toward cooperative defense and development of the area. The concept of common interests among the islands and their people was slow in gaining a foothold among the opinion makers in the area. At present, elements of that group are showing an increased awareness of common interests, but the concept has barely begun to take root among the people themselves. The once promising West Indies Federation failed to gain the official and popular support necessary to permit it to continue.

At the Fifth Seminar this background was well portrayed in a paper on "Patterns and Problems of Publishing in the Caribbean Area" by David K. Easton, who had formerly served as Librarian for the Caribbean Commission. He noted that in addition to the islands he was including the three Guianas, since they shared the same economic, social, and cultural problems. Bibliographic tasks were difficult everywhere in the area. Many of the problems were common to Latin America but were intensified in the Caribbean. Additional ones were created by the diversity of linguistic backgrounds and political ties and traditions. With regard to publishing he said in part:

> The modern publisher is defined as one who produces books and places them on the market. It is not the usual practice in Europe and the U.S. for the business of publisher and printer to be joined. In the

West Indies, with the exception of Puerto Rico and Cuba, and perhaps Haiti, creative writing usually appears in print exclusively as the result of the efforts of the author. The printer usually assumes only the responsibilities of editing and publishing compilations such as directories and almanacs or other annuals which have proved their marketability through the years.

He stated that since 1948 the most active publisher in the area had been the Caribbean Commission. Of its origins he said:

In 1942 the Anglo-American Commission was created to deal jointly with the acute problems common to both nations. This may be considered the initiation of planning directed towards community of effort in the West Indies. The Dutch were drawn towards the organization by requirements of defense although they did not join the Commission until 1946. The French territories, which had been isolated during the War by the Vichy government of Admiral Roberts in Martinique, also joined in 1946. The organization then became the Caribbean Commission.

The Caribbean Commission as instituted in 1946 was a consultative and advisory body only, with four-power representation. Its headquarters were in Trinidad. The most important single publication of the Commission was its monthly bulletin, *The Caribbean,* published from 1947 through April 1960. Bibliographic information was an important feature. Its distribution was somewhat limited—as was the roster of institutions with any special interest in the Caribbean and complete sets are now scarce.

Some of the most lasting benefits of the Caribbean Commission are due to its creation of a library, which, fortunately, was headed at critical points by able individuals endowed with vision and energy. Since the main objective of the Commission was the furthering of the economic and social well-being of the area, to which end it would concern itself with matters of common interest—particularly agriculture, communications, education, fishing, health, housing, industry, labor, social welfare, and trade—the need for a reference and research library was obvious.

Once the Library of the Caribbean Commission was organized, the need for a bibliographic record of such printed materials as it was able to acquire from the area also became evident. In 1951 it published the first issue of what was originally intended to be a quarterly record: *Current Caribbean Bibliography.* Its subtitle declared it to be "an alphabetical list of publications issued in the Caribbean territories of France, Great Britain, the Netherlands, and the United States." The last issue for 1953 was a cumulative one from 1950 to date, and from 1954 publication was intended to be on an annual basis. Volume 8, 1959, cumulating 1954-1958 listings, was the last number published during the lifetime of the Commission. In 1959 the Caribbean Commission terminated its existence as such. It was superseded in 1960 by the Caribbean Organization, representing the same four "metropolitan powers" as its predecessor, but with headquarters in Hato Rey, Puerto Rico (a suburb of San Juan).

Matters concerning the Caribbean Commission stood at this point when the Fifth Seminar convened in New York in June 1960. Two outstanding participants from the Caribbean area were Enid M. Baa, then Chief of the Bureau of Libraries and Museums of the Virgin Islands of the United States, and William E. Gocking, then Librarian of the University College of the West Indies (Jamaica.) Miss Baa presented a paper on "Inter-Library Cooperation and Its Relation to Problems of Acquisition of Library Materials from the Caribbean Islands" and Mr. Gocking one on "Exchange of Publications in the [British] West Indies."

Miss Baa's paper was a well-organized and informative one. It provided brief descriptions of the existing libraries and library services in the major islands, most of which she had visited in person, and it is still useful. She noted that at the Fourth Seminar (1959) she had "dared to point out the great necessity for a Conference of Caribbean librarians, archivests, and information officers." She stated that the idea had been initiated and supported by the Caribbean Commission since 1952, but that with each successive year it had been postponed and by then seemed impossible.

Some months later Miss Baa was named the Librarian of the Caribbean Organization and was granted a leave of absence from her post in the Virgin Islands. She moved to Puerto Rico where she gave outstanding service to the development of library techniques and cooperation in the area until the Caribbean Organization voted in December 1964 to terminate its existence as of June 30, 1965. She then returned to the Virgin Islands, from which base she has continued to make important contributions to SALALM in general and to bibliographical services in particular.

Mr. Gocking's paper (which was, for reasons stated, hastily prepared) presented some interesting viewpoints and important facts. When he, the Librarian of what was then the University College of the West Indies (but which has since become the University of the West Indies, with campuses in Trinidad and Barbados as well as Jamaica), used the term "West Indies," he was speaking of the English-speaking islands only. He has continued to be a leading spokesman for the very important units of the area formerly known as the British West Indies. With reference to *Current Caribbean Bibliography,* he said:

> It lists its publications in three classes: periodicals and newspapers, Government serials, and monographs. It should be a most useful guide for all those interested in acquiring West Indian publications. ... It must be added, however, that the mere listing of a publication is no guarantee that it can be obtained. West Indian bookselling ... is still, as they say today, underdeveloped.

With this background laid, the long and complicated story of bibliographic developments in the area during the rest of the decade can only be sketched here. It has been partially told in SALALM papers and conference reports. There have been important results and there are great possibilities, but at this point there are also great uncertainties.

As a result of the papers and discussions of the Fifth Seminar, a meeting of the SALALM Subcommittee on Caribbean Bibliography was held at the Lucerne Hotel, Miami Beach, on April 27, 1961, "to explore the possibilities of achieving an 'integrated bibliography' of the Caribbean Area." It was thought that the presence of the Caribbean Organization in Hato Rey, a San Juan suburb near the University of Puerto Rico and its recently established Institute of Caribbean Studies, would make possible more current and comprehensive coverage of bibliographic information than had been possible up until that time.

Miss Baa, as Librarian for the Caribbean Organization, had pointed out that the chronic difficulties of producing the *Current Caribbean Bibliography* came largely from the fact that no financial provision had ever been made for its preparation, but only for its publication once an overburdened staff had assembled and edited the data. She favored the establishment of a documentation center to include not only a library and bibliographic service, but photoreproduction facilities and translation and interlibrary loan services.

A prerequisite for obtaining adequate bibliographical data was the fundamental one of securing the publications themselves from the diverse and extensive Caribbean area, whether by some such plan as the Stechert-Hafner LACAP program or by some other method. Participants in the meeting agreed that many of the problems inherent in the situation could be resolved by a bibliographic center which would have a seven-point set of objectives. It was clear that personnel would have to be trained in the various islands, that periodic visits by center personnel would be required, and that modern techniques would have to be utilized to produce a com-

prehensive and current bibliography. Such a center, when and if established, might well serve as a model for possible adaptation elsewhere in
Latin America. It was decided to seek funds (which were later obtained
from the American Library Association's Council on Library Resources) to
send Marietta Daniels and Robert Kingery to Puerto Rico to discuss possibilities for cooperation among the several interested institutions.

As a result of the visit of Daniels and Kingery to Puerto Rico and of
subsequent action by the Sixth Seminar, (1961), Miss Daniels prepared a
memorandum, "Proposal for an Inter-American Bibliographic Institute to
be Initiated by a Pilot Center for Bibliographic Information for the Caribbean," dated September 28, 1961. In 1963 she prepared and distributed
"An Inter-American Bibliographic Institute: a Proposal for Comprehensive
International Bibliographic and Cataloging Control."

At the Eighth Seminar (1963) Miss Baa presented a paper, "Library and
Bibliographic Activities in the Caribbean." It was a factual and well-
organized compilation of information which, although now partially out-
dated, is not likely soon to be superseded. For present purposes, however,
the most important part was her prefatory observations concerning the
area. She re-emphasized the problems of diversity of backgrounds and of
cultural ties with countries outside the area, and the fact that most of the
important works by Caribbean authors were published outside the area—in
Europe, the United States, or Latin America. Local publications were
difficult to secure because (1) there was no way to know what was published, (2) there was no central agency from which to secure desired items
that were known, and (3) current bibliographies or publishers' catalogs
were not available. She considered that the place where these problems
could best be discussed and solutions found would be a "library development conference" or "seminar for the Caribbean area," for which financial
assistance would be provided by the Department of Education of the
Commonwealth of Puerto Rico and the Government of the Virgin Islands
of the United States. The date was to be determined by the Caribbean
Council at its meeting in September 1963. (Unfortunately the Council of
the Caribbean Organization failed to take the necessary action.)

By this time Miss Baa, as Librarian of the Caribbean Organization and
Chairman of the SALALM ad hoc Committee for the Establishing of a
Caribbean Bibliographic Center, was conferring in Puerto Rico with systems analysts and was preparing estimates as to the costs of operating the
proposed center. Various agencies were approached for funds, but without
favorable results. There the matter rested at the time of the demise of the
Caribbean Organization, in June 1965.

The exceptional nature of the Library of the Caribbean Organization was sufficiently recognized for a number of institutions and agencies to make known their interest in acquiring it. The final decision was to leave it in trust to the Commonwealth of Puerto Rico unless and until some successor international organization representing the area should be created. The Library was to be under the jurisdiction of a newly created Comisión para el Desarrollo Económico del Caribe, commonly known by the derived term CODECA. The Library was to maintain its integrity and to be available for service, primarily to the area formerly comprising the Organization. It was to be known thenceforth as the Caribbean Regional Library. The CODECA charter, as granted by the Commonwealth's Legislature, undertook not only to maintain the Library but also:

(1) To bring up to date as soon as possible *Current Caribbean Bibliography* and to continue its publication and circulation on a more extensive basis, utilizing the most modern methods and techniques of information gathering and dissemination and
(2) To seek assistance from all possible sources to increase the value, efficiency, and service ability of the Library.

The Librarian named to head the Caribbean Regional Library, Miss Paulita C. Maldonado (who later became Mrs. Paulita C. Maldonado de la Torre), had had several years of experience in the New York area. Named as Executive Director of CODECA was Dr. Luis A. Passalacqua, who did all in his power to further the interests of the Library.

Developments within the next few months included the following: A cooperative agreement was reached in November 1966 between CODECA and the University of Puerto Rico's Institute of Caribbean Studies for the preparation of the volumes of *Current Caribbean Bibliography,* for which data had been collected but not assembled and edited. The Institute was to prepare the volumes for 1965-1966 so that the Caribbean Regional Library could concentrate on preparing Part II of the volume covering the years 1959-1961 and the one for 1962-1964. Once the back volumes were provided, the CRL expected to be able to prepare a 1967 volume by automated procedures and from then on to keep production on a really current basis. CODECA issued a press release dated January 3, 1967, stating that the Caribbean Regional Library had contracted for the services of the System Development Corporation to survey the Library's operations and to assist in the designing of a bibliographic center.

Frequent discussions and planning sessions were held by Puerto Rican librarians on ways and means of helping establish the center. A Conference on the Establishment of a Regional Bibliographic Center for the Caribbean was held at the headquarters of CODECA, the host organization, on March 27-29, 1967.* Miss Enid Baa, Librarian during the period of the Caribbean Organization (1960-1965), was elected presiding officer. The Conference brought together a strong representation from the English-speaking West Indies and the Netherlands West Indies as well as from Puerto Rico, and guests from particularly concerned Mainland institutions and from Denmark—the last named because of the special relationship of the Virgin Islands of the United States to that country. Among the Mainland participants was the then Senior Vice President of University Microfilms, Inc., a Xerox company, who had been approached by the SALALM Committee on Bibliography concerning the possibility of installing Xerox facilities at as low a cost as possible in order to make available to other libraries or to research workers the valuable holdings of the Caribbean Regional Library, some of which are unique and many of which are irreplaceable.

An account of the situation as of mid-1967, together with a useful background sketch of the project, was given to the Twelfth Seminar by Mrs. Maldonado de la Torre in a paper entitled "Considerations in the Development of a Caribbean Regional Collection." She noted that the survey completed by the System Development Corporation early in 1967 had showed that the Library had in fact been performing some of the functions of a bibliographic center since 1951 when the first issue of *Current Caribbean Bibliography* was published. However, its effectiveness as such had always been limited by available resources and outside influences. The survey stressed the cooperative aspects of the program and its importance to the area, but also stressed the facts that plans were "necessarily projections across time and, in an effort of this magnitude, they [were] directly related to the availability of funds, trained personnel, and cooperation in the entire Caribbean community."

The study of the System Development Corporation indicated that the first step would necessarily be the implementation of an "interim capability" of the Caribbean Regional Library by improving its procedures and its products within its working limitations, so that it would become able and ready to perform the functions of a bibliographic center. The Library would assume financial responsibility for the interim capability and would

---

* A full report of the Conference was published in the Official Records series of the Caribbean Economic Development Corporation as document number 064.2/1/67/E, March 1967 (handwritten notation on copy at hand). A résumé is contained in the "Progress Report" of the Permanent Secretary of SALALM, Marietta Daniels Shepard, to the Twelfth Seminar (Section II, pp. 28-29).

begin work on it by July of that year (1967). CODECA would seek financial assistance to implement the full program. The recommendations of the study included the completion of arrangements with the computing center of the University of Puerto Rico for the keypunching of "entry worksheets" and for the use of its computer to print the punch-card file on multilith masters, so as to be able to publish *Current Caribbean Bibliography* and interim lists for distribution. The first of the new printout lists had been distributed under date of March 1967 to participants at the Conference on the Establishment of a Regional Bibliographic Center for the Caribbean.

At the Thirteenth Seminar (1968) the Progress Report of the Permanent Secretary of the Seminars, Marietta Daniels Shepard, included a report on the Caribbean Regional Library as submitted by the Director of the CRL. Hopes of the previous year for securing funds to make the proposed pilot Bibliographic Center for the Caribbean operational had not materialized, but some real achievements could be reported.

Among the more significant advances made, with the assistance of the System Development Corporation, was the completion of the procedures for preparing the staff to receive, process, and disseminate bibliographic information on materials published in or about the Caribbean. At the end of a four-month contract period with the SDC, the Caribbean Regional Library had a sophisticated system in operation, of which four characteristics were listed. One, "a revised worksheet containing all elements of bibliographic information now in use by the Library which is compatible with MARC,"* had been discussed at the Conference on the Establishment of a Regional Bibliographic Center for the Caribbean. It was realized that the procedure would involve additional training of personnel in the contributing libraries of the islands or the Mainland, but it was considered very much worthwhile. The worksheet as developed was reported "capable of handling additional elements without major revision." Also, a computer program was to be worked out to make it possible to prepare *Current Caribbean Bibliography* on an annual basis "and a bimonthly supplement to be produced via computer processing."

Altogether, the "interim capability" stage had been completed by January 1, 1968, so that the CRL was ready to "enter fully into the develop-

---

* "MARC" represents the Machine Readable Catalog Project of the Library of Congress. Two recent important books concerning it are: *The MARC Pilot Project; Final Report...* prepared by Henriette D. Auram, Washington, Library of Congress, 1968, 183 p., $3.50, and *MARC Manuals Used by the Library of Congress,* prepared by the Informations Systems Office, Library of Congress, Chicago, American Library Association, 1969, 335 p., $7.50.

ment of the regional bibliographic center." (That simple statement indicates a landmark of tremendous importance to bibliographic standards and possibilities not only in the Caribbean but potentially in all of Latin America!) An important development was the bimonthly computer-produced *Supplement* to *Current Caribbean Bibliography* (now on a monthly basis), which had become a union list to the extent that acquisitions were promptly reported by eight participating institutions. Of the back volumes of the *CCB*, volumes 9-11 (Part 2) for 1959-1961 and volume 15 for 1965 had been issued. They were prepared respectively by the CRL and by the UPR's Institute of Caribbean Studies, but both were being distributed by the CRL. Of the other volumes lacking, numbers 12-14 (1962-1964) were under preparation by the CRL and volume 16 by the Institute.

The photocopying of materials was a further service which the CRL had become capable of rendering. It was reported to the Thirteenth Seminar that earlier conversations with University Microfilms had proved fruitful and that a staff member of CRL had been sent to Ann Arbor to be trained in the operations involved in the microfilming and copying of materials. As of February 1, 1968, the service had become operational—another step towards rendering bibliographic center services.

At the Thirteenth Seminar a tentative decision was made to hold the next meeting in Puerto Rico in June 1969, with the Caribbean Regional Library under CODECA auspices serving as host. When a firm decision to do so was reached, the Caribbean library world entered a period of intense activity. The three months prior to the convening of the Fourteenth Seminar saw a series of conferences, each of which was of value and served to bring together varying portions of the area personnel who were especially concerned with developing its bibliographical resources. Always there was present the question of how first to secure and identify materials (primarily books and pamphlets) so that a bibliographical record could be made—it was hoped while the materials were still available.

The series of international library conferences in the Caribbean was led off by a Conference on Sharing Caribbean Resources for Study and Research, held at the College of the Virgin Islands, St. Thomas, on March 17-19, immediately following the dedication of the CVI's new Ralph M. Paiewonsky Library. Participants were chiefly from the Caribbean, including, happily, representatives from the Dominican Republic and the French and Dutch islands. Present also were guests from institutions with strong Caribbean interests in England, Denmark, Holland, and the United States. It is expected that the proceedings will be published by the CVI.

From April 30 to May 1 a Conference on Inter-Library Cooperation was held in Puerto Rico. Its function was largely preparatory and participants were almost exclusively from the local area. A report of this Conference was being edited by the CRL as of September 1969.

Finally, announcement was made that the First Caribbean Conference on University and Research Institute Cooperation would take place in Puerto Rico on June 14-17, immediately prior to the Fourteenth Seminar, to be held at the same location (the Condado Beach Hotel). Such a conference, envisioned earlier by Enid Baa as Librarian of the Caribbean Organization (who stated that UNESCO had been stressing the need for a regional conference since 1952), toward which Paulita Maldonado de la Torre had worked since the initiation of the Caribbean Regional Library in 1966, was finally called by Dr. Alma Jordan, Deputy Librarian of the University of the West Indies at St. Augustine, Trinidad. That it could then be held was due to a major new development in the Caribbean area, the formation of an Association of Caribbean Universities,* whose Executive Director is appropriately Sir Philip Sherlock, the former Deputy Chancellor of the University of the West Indies.

It was with great anticipation that participants gathered in Puerto Rico for the weekend pre-SALALM Conference. Much was accomplished, most notably organization of the group on a permanent basis, to be known as ACURIL, acronym for the Association of Caribbean University and Research Institute Libraries. Dr. Alma Jordan was elected President of the Association, with supporting officers from Puerto Rico and an Executive Council of six from various locations. ACURIL is to meet annually in the Caribbean. Its objectives include the cooperative acquisition of library material for the area and cooperative bibliographic and indexing projects.†

The pre-SALALM Conference was clouded, as was SALALM also, when participants learned that the future of the Caribbean Regional Library was·

---

* The official organ of the Association is the *Caribbean Educational Bulletin*, which is prepared and distributed by the Institute for Caribbean Studies, University of Puerto Rico, Río Piedras. The issue for September 1969 features ACURIL, the librarians' conference. (The numbering, "vol. 6, no. 11," is that of the now defunct *Caribbean Bulletin*, distributed until recently by the Institute of Caribbean Studies.) An article providing some account of the background of the Association of Caribbean Universities and of events leading up to the June 1969 conference of librarians, by this writer, appeared in the *South Eastern Latin Americanist, Quarterly Journal of the South Eastern Conference on Latin American Studies,* for June 1969 (13:1, pp. 1-4).

† "Report on the First Caribbean Conference on University and Research Institute Library Cooperation held in San Juan, Puerto Rico, June 14-17, 1969" by Donald F. Wisdom, in the Library of Congress Information Bulletin for July 3, 1969 (Appendix II, pp. 350-51), provides a brief account.

in some doubt because of the uncertainty as to the future of CODECA, whose charter had provided for continued support of the CRL. The reason was that the first change in many years in party control in Puerto Rico was bringing organizational changes. Representatives of the Puerto Rican government had given assurances that the obligations undertaken by it when the Commonwealth was chosen as the agency to which the Caribbean Organization's library was awarded in trust would be honored. The assurances had not been forthcoming in time, unfortunately, to prevent the resignation of the Director of the CRL, Mrs. Maldonado de la Torre, to accept another position. In spite of this crisis situation, the personnel of the CRL, aided by representatives of the University of Puerto Rico Library and of the Institute of Caribbean Studies, met admirably their obligations as the host organizations.

Mr. Joseph J. Breen, formerly with the System Development Corporation, had been re-employed by the CRL to bring the Library's automated procedures to the point of meeting fully the goals set for the "interim capacity" stage—that of being able, when funds for services could be provided, to serve not only the demands made upon the Library as such, but for it to render bibliographical services to the entire Caribbean community. These services would be on a cooperative basis, dependent largely upon information provided by libraries from other islands or countries and even better from book materials sent directly to the CRL.

Progress in the state of the art in the two years after the Conference in March 1967 for the Establishment of a Regional Bibliographic Center for the Caribbean at the CRL was extraordinary. Most visible evidence was the fact that the printout supplements to *Current Caribbean Bibliography* were being published monthly and had become a union list—within the limits of information submitted in time to be included in the first monthly list noting the item, since it would otherwise automatically be eliminated as a duplicate entry. Participating institutions, as represented by the code list for all libraries known to have "at least one copy of the announced item," were the following:

CRL	Caribbean Regional Library, Puerto Rico
IN	Institute of Jamaica, Jamaica
LC	Library of Congress, Washington, D.C.
NAC	Netherlands Antilles, Curaçao
UFG	University of Florida, Gainesville
UNPHU	Universidad Nacional Pedro Henríquez Ureña, Dominican Republic
UPR	University of Puerto Rico, Puerto Rico

USVI   United States Virgin Islands
UWIJ   University of the West Indies, Jamaica
UWIT   University of the West Indies, Trinidad

The Caribbean Regional Library had met its original commitment to publish the delayed volumes of *Current Caribbean Bibliography,* leaving only volumes 12/14 for 1962/1964, and volume 16 for 1966 of the pre-automated period to be published. Responsibility for these had been assumed by the Institute of Caribbean Studies and much work had been done on them. The Institute had lost the services of the librarian in charge of the project, Luisa Vigo-Cepeda, and further delay was possible, but the volumes would definitely appear to complete the set through 1966.

This record of cooperative achievement and the bright prospects for the initiation of a Regional Bibliographic Center on at least a step-by-step basis should have been an occasion for celebration at this first meeting of SALALM in the Caribbean area, but rejoicing over the advances in the state of the art and the benefits expected to flow therefrom was overshadowed by the uncertainties of the situation. The CRL was continuing to function with Mrs. Ana Mercedes L. de González (a well-informed assistant to the former Director) as Acting Director, but its future had not been resolved as of December 1969. Added to these uncertainties were others in cooperating institutions. The Institute of Caribbean Studies changed directors at midyear. However, the incoming Director, Dr. H. Hoetink, who had formerly been associated with the Institute, could be expected to continue its cooperation. A very different matter was the astounding information reported to the library world in September 1969 that the Director of the Library of the University of Puerto Rico, Miss Josefina del Toro, who had with her staff given full cooperation to both ACURIL and SALALM at a time when the Library was under strain because of a building program and increased demands, had been dismissed on June 30 with only a few hours notice and had been superseded by a faculty member with no training in librarianship and no administrative experience![*]

Altogether, what should here be a climactic announcement concerning the state of the art with respect to the extremely important Caribbean Regional Library and its condition of readiness to become a regional bibliographical center must be reported instead as a decision which hangs in the balance. Sponsorship and continued cooperation of neighboring institutions are the crucial matters. After all the storms that have been weathered

* *Library Journal,* September 15, 1969, p. 2992.

previously, the present situation seems almost a "Perils of Pauline" melo-drama, which must surely have a happy ending. Would that there were such assurance!

PUERTO RICO

The Commonwealth of Puerto Rico benefits in various ways from its dual heritage. An important example is its educational system up to and includ-ing expanding graduate programs. In August 1969 a graduate school of librarianship began its first year of operation. Housed in new quarters at the University of Puerto Rico, it gives promise of filling an island-wide need for additional qualified librarians in schools, colleges, and public libraries and incidentally of expanding the already considerable amount of bibliographic expertise available in the Commonwealth. It is hoped that, through the training of students from other countries, the new school will have a leavening influence upon the entire area.

Previous to the time when the University could offer a master's degree in library science, scholarships were provided to enable students to study at Mainland universities. Consequently, while Puerto Rico has not had all the librarians it needs, it has had a few outstanding ones for many years and an increasing number of capable and energetic ones. Prominent among the earlier stalwarts are two who earned their library science degrees in the thirties at Columbia University, Gonzalo Velázquez in 1934 and Josefina del Toro about 1937.

The latter's *Bibliography of the Collective Biography of Spanish Amer-ica,* published by the University of Puerto Rico in 1938, has not yet been superseded, and as Director of the Central Library Miss del Toro was largely responsible for the planning of the recently expanded library build-ing, with quarters for the library school. Of the various Puerto Rican librarians mentioned elsewhere as contributors to SALALM or for other activities—notably in connection with the Caribbean Regional Library, the Institute of Caribbean Studies, or ACURIL—almost all have worked with or studied under Miss del Toro at the UPR at some time and hold advanced degrees from Mainland universities.

The UPR Central Library serves the Institute of Caribbean Studies, which does not maintain a separate collection. The invaluable "Current Bibliography" section in *Caribbean Studies,* the official journal of the Institute of Caribbean Studies, has been prepared by a succession of espe-cially capable bibliographers who have held the title of Librarian of Latin

American Studies—Antonio Matos, Dr. Albertina Pérez de Rosa, and, beginning in 1969, Mrs. María Elena Argüello de Cardona. The stated purpose of "Current Bibliography" is "to make immediately available the titles of current books, pamphlets, and articles of interest to Caribbeanists. The Caribbean is defined as comprising the Antilles, Yucatán, British Honduras, Central America, Panama, Colombia, Venezuela, and the Guianas." Completeness and accuracy are aspired to, but really *current* bibliography "seems especially important in a region in which locally published items are soon out of print."

In terms of subject matter, *Caribbean Studies*, including its numerous book reviews and "Current Bibliography," is limited to the social sciences and the humanities. A companion periodical, *Caribbean Journal of Science*, is published on the Mayagüez campus of the University, and provides some bibliographical data covering publications in scientific fields for Puerto Rico and elsewhere in the region, but not on a comparable basis.

As would be expected, the best current record of publications from or about Puerto Rico is provided by "Current Bibliography." This is the more true since the UPR maintains a Puerto Rican collection which aims to be as comprehensive as possible. In accordance with the usual pattern, books and pamphlets are listed in one section and periodical articles in another.

There is no provision for the cumulation of the data supplied by the two Caribbean journals as such, but Puerto Rico has been fortunate in having an annual bibliography, separately prepared. Its *Anuario bibliográfico puertorriqueño*, first published in 1948, is, like the bibliographical records produced in Cuba and Haiti during the same period, the work of one individual bibliographer. Gonzalo Velázquez compiled the *Anuario* for 1948-1952 while on the staff of the UPR, and the first four volumes were published by the University. Since that time he has been the Director of Bibliographic Services of the Department of Education, and the *Anuario* has been irregularly published. Sr. Velázquez is an assiduous bibliographer and continues to maintain up-to-date files. However, his numerous duties and the heavy demands upon the publishing facilities of the Department of Education have prevented the *Anuario*'s appearing promptly for several years. Until 1969 the latest volume generally distributed was for 1956. A handsome, 389-page volume covering 1959/60 was distributed in 1969 to participants in the Fourteenth Seminar during its meeting at San Juan. However, it bears a colophon date of November 25, 1966.

The *Anuario* is, as described by its subtitle, an alphabetical list of books, pamphlets, periodicals, and newspapers published in Puerto Rico during the period indicated. It is alphabetical in the "dictionary catalog" sense, and a work may appear under author, subject, and title. Extensive lists of government publications are included. In short, as national bibliography, the *Anuario bibliográfico puertorriqueño* is an excellent example of the bibliographer's art and as such does great credit to Puerto Rico, but, unfortunately, it is not, at present, *current* bibliography.

A partial substitute for the *Anuario bibliográfico puertorriqueño* is provided by *Current Caribbean Bibliography* and by its monthly *Supplements*, which are fully described in the section on the Caribbean in general. However, the annual cumulations of *CCB* are still not fully up to date, and in any case the bibliographical approach is on a subject rather than a regional basis. The computer printout *Supplements* produced in 1969, which show what library provided the data, indicate the extensive contributions of the UPR Library.

The UPR Library and the Institute of Caribbean Studies have cooperated extensively with the Caribbean Regional Library, under its CODECA (Comisión para el Desarrollo Económico del Caribe) sponsorship, both in bibliographical matters and in sharing responsibility for the hosting of international conferences, such as the ACURIL and SALALM conferences of June 1969.

Summary

Puerto Rico has been able, largely through its association with the United States, to develop a corps of able librarians, prepared professionally at the best schools of librarianship on the Mainland. Results are evident (1) in the excellent contributions to current national bibliography in *Caribbean Studies*, (2) in its *Anuario bibliográfico puertorriqueño* (now nearly a decade behind date), and (3) in cooperative efforts towards the development and support of the Caribbean Regional Library under CODECA auspices. The inauguration of a graduate school of librarianship at the UPR in August 1969 should, among other things and over a period of time, contribute toward the raising of the standards of national bibliography throughout the Hispanic Caribbean and the circum-Caribbean countries.

CUBA

Cuba's record in the hemisphere with regard to its national bibliography is unique in various ways. Its *Anuario bibliográfico cubano,* or, to use the later title, *Bibliografía cubana,* covered a long period, 1937-1965, and was primarily the work of one man. It owed its inception to a recommendation of an International Conference of American States—the Seventh, which met in Montevideo in 1933, and which is memorable for various reasons, chiefly as the occasion on which the United States accepted the principle of nonintervention. Among Conference recommendations was one to the effect that each of the American countries should regularly compile and make available for distribution among its sister republics the record of its current publications, as an essential basis for self-knowledge and for mutual understanding.

In Cuba a young man who was appointed in that same year to be the Director of the Municipal Library of Havana, Fermín Peraza y Sarausa (1907-1969), took the injunction seriously and set to work. In 1938 he published the first volume of his *Anuario bibliográfico cubano*, listing publications for 1937. It continued to appear as such until 1953, when the title was changed to *Bibliografía cubana*. In 1961 it celebrated its "Bodas de plata," although by that time Peraza and his wife had departed Cuba, first for Medellín, Colombia, and then to Gainesville, Florida, where both became members of the staff of the University of Florida Library.

That Dr. Peraza was able to continue to assemble more data concerning current Cuban publications than was any other agency during the early years of the sixties was due largely to his own assiduous pursuit of information. But the aid he received from former students of his course in Cuban bibliography at the University of Havana, sometimes by clandestine means, contributed towards the completeness of the compilation. The final volume of his annual account of Cuban publications, begun in 1937, set an unmatched record for the continuous assembling, editing, and publishing of a country's current national bibliography by one person. His *Bibliografía cubana, 1965,* was published by him in Gainesville, Florida, in 1966.

Revolutionary Cuba: a Bibliographical Guide, an English language record covering 1966, compiled by Dr. Peraza at the University of Miami and published by its Press in 1967, took a somewhat different approach. The 695 items consisted mainly of books, pamphlets, and leaflets published in or about Cuba in 1966, but included some analytic references to relevant sections of books. Part of the value of *Revolutionary Cuba* lies in its extensive inclusion of materials published outside Cuba, particularly in the United States and especially in the Miami area. The volumes for 1967 and 1968 were reported in press when he died, January 31, 1969.*

* The 1967 volume, listing 911 items, was distributed late in 1969. A preface, signed by Mose L. Harvey, Director of the Center for Advanced International Studies, University of Miami, and dated May 14, 1969, indicated the Center's expectation that the work would be

A valuable compilation, specifically devoted to periodical publications by Cuban exiles, has been made by Rosa M. Abella, who contributed to the Eleventh Seminar (1966) a paper on "Publicaciones periódicas editadas en el exilio y en existencia en la Biblioteca de la Universidad de Miami." She provided supplements for the Thirteenth and Fourteenth Seminars.

Fidel Castro and his immediate predecessor, Fulgencio Batista, shared at least one admirable characteristic—a high regard for libraries. It was under Batista that the Biblioteca Nacional Jose Martí was constructed as an important part of the governmental complex of buildings at the Plaza de la Revolución. The choice of Havana as the seat of the Regional Center for UNESCO in the Western Hemisphere early in the 1950s had given new impetus to libraries and bibliographical activities, already thriving. It had been as the head of the Grupo Bibliográfico Nacional José Toribio Medina that Fermín Peraza had served as the Technical Director for the *Bibliografía de Centroamérica y del Caribe,* 1956-1959.

Cuba entered the Castro era, then, fully equipped with bibliographic skills to compile the national bibliography. Given a controlled system of publishing, a centralized state control of the book trade, what was presumably the best observed law of legal deposit in the Western hemisphere, and library personnel able and eager to make known to the world both publications by Cubans and those about Cuba, it was only a matter of time until a national bibliography under the auspices of the Biblioteca Nacional would be forthcoming.

The first volume of *Bibliografía cubana,* prepared in the Biblioteca Nacional and published by the Consejo Nacional de Cultura, covered 1963/1964 and bore a colophon date of March 27, 1967. The volume for 1965 appeared also in 1967, and the one for 1959-1962 was dated February 7, 1968. In the summer of 1968 the 1966 volume was published, thereby approaching currency on an annual basis. The introduction to the 1959-1962 volume observed that the centenary of the birth of the greatest of Cuban bibliographers, Carlos Manuel Trelles y Govín (1866-1951) had recently been celebrated, and that Cuba was greatly indebted to him for his incomparable *Bibliografía cubana,* spanning the whole period of publishing in Cuba from the seventeenth century until 1917. A gap existed until 1937 when the *Anuario bibliográfico cubano* began its coverage. The introduction, signed only "Colección cubana, Biblioteca Nacional 'José Martí,'" noted that by 1961 the difficult task of assembling the record of

---

continued. Recent information is that Elena V. Peraza, Dr. Peraza's widow and until his death his close collaborator, is continuing the compilation. For the present, at least, this task is in addition to her full-time duties as a cataloguer in the University of Miami Library.

publications in Cuba from 1959-1962 had been undertaken. Many publications had appeared without dates, which bibliographers had had to deduce from context or circumstances as best they could. An attempt was made to include foreign publications about Cuba, so far as it was possible under existing international circumstances for Cuban libraries to secure either the publications or data concerning them. The result was a 2,776-item bibliography, arranged by subject under a list of 77 topics, with full bibliographic data and with an author index, including also some titles and subjects. An "Indice cronológico" simply lists many rows of the numbers of items referred to. The same arrangement, except for the chronological index, has been followed in later volumes.

For up-to-date coverage, the best source for Cuban bibliography at present is "Current Bibliography" in the quarterly issues of *Caribbean Studies.*

Summary

Cuba's unique bibliographical history is one of nearly unbroken coverage from the colonial period to the present, a record unsurpassed in Latin America. The only gap is the interval between 1917, the terminal date of the coverage by Carlos M. Trelles y Govín and 1937, the beginning of the more than 30-year period covered by Fermín Peraza. For the years 1959-1966 there is now double coverage. The Peraza *Bibliografía cubana* and for 1966 *Revolutionary Cuba* cover those years, as does also the *Bibliografía cubana* by the Biblioteca Nacional José Martí. In 1967 and 1968 the latter brought out four volumes covering in sequence 1963/1964, 1965, 1959/1962, and 1966. The double coverage will presumably be extended indefinitely, provided the continued publication of *Revolutionary Cuba* proves possible.

It seems safe to say that no other Latin American country could have exported as much bibliographical talent as did Cuba during the 1960s and still retain enough to compile its national bibliography for that decade and to bring its publication to a state approaching currency by the end of the period.

DOMINICAN REPUBLIC

The Dominican Republic has lacked a real national bibliography, but it seems quite possible that one may be produced in the not too distant future. The background situation is an outstanding example, among many in Latin America, of the results of the efforts of one person and of his continuing influence. In the valuable paper on "Library and Bibliographic Activities in the Dominican Republic," prepared by Enid M. Baa and Ligia Espinal de Hoetink for the Ninth Seminar (1964), the authors noted the credit due Dr. Luis Florén Lozano, who had devoted his energies to the preparation of library personnel before accepting the Directorship of the Inter-American School of Library Science, in Medellín, Colombia. (His training had been in Spain, which he left as an émigré following the Spanish Civil War.)

The authors noted that professional librarians were scarce except at the University Library, where all librarians interviewed had trained under Dr. Florén Lozano when he directed the Library, beginning about 1942. Of the first class of five graduated from his course in library science, two are of particular importance to the Dominican Republic's bibliographic records. Dr. Próspero Mella Chavier, who was "considered the best authority on librarianship in the country," had been, we may note, the *compilador nacional* who had reported to the *Bibliografía de Centroamérica y del Caribe* for the years 1956-1958, the three in which the Dominican Republic was represented. During those years he provided the data also to the *Anales de la Universidad de Santo Domingo,* which included them as removable supplements.

Sra. Rosa Elena Despradel Batista, who was also ranked high for her contributions, had become by 1969 the Director of the General Library of the Autonomous University of Santo Domingo and as such was its representative to the First Conference on University and Research Institute Library Cooperation (ACURIL), held in Puerto Rico on June 14-17, 1969. Sra. Despradel indicated at the Conference that plans were under way to begin the publication of a bibliographic bulletin, perhaps with a cumulated annual edition.

The UASD Library has for years attempted to collect all publications possible from and about the Dominican Republic, and some time ago it was officially designated as the depository for all authors who want copyright protection. It appears that such protection is lightly esteemed there, as in so many other Latin American countries, and many, if not most, works are unregistered. However, the University Library has had an active acquisitions program for some years, and its collection is the strongest one on national materials in the country, with the possible exception of extraordinary private collections. (The National Archive has a strong collection of archival materials, but that is a different story.) A National Library is reported to be under construction, with 1970 set for completion.

Meanwhile, the UASD Library has, in fact, begun publication of the promised bulletin. The first issue of the mimeographed *Boletín de adquisiciones,* bearing a stamped date of September 1969, was received from Sra. Despradel early in December. A letter states that it is to be published bimonthly. The *Boletín,* which is prepared primarily for the information of the University community as to available materials, includes a section on "Libros dominicanos." The section contains 51 full bibliographic entries for books from or about the country, chiefly 1967-1969 publications. There is a 24-item list of recent publications of the University covering about the same period.

Sra. Despradel enclosed also copies of the mimeographed acquisitions list from the recently founded Universidad Católica Madre y Maestra. Another new university, the Universidad Nacional Pedro Henríquez Ureña, began publication of its library bulletin *Biblio-notas* in June 1967, very soon after the date of its own founding—April of that year. A foreword indicated that the main function of the bulletin was to acquaint faculty and students with the materials available to them. The June 1968 issue was devoted to acquisitions from or about the country. This bulletin is arranged by large topics, such as Economics and Literature, while the former is arranged by the Dewey Decimal System. Both include lists of periodicals received. Such bulletins serve their primary purpose more or less well, as they do also a secondary purpose of providing current information to interested national institutions or persons and to exchange partners elsewhere. However, the long-term reference value of such bulletins is minimal, especially if the proportion of national materials is relatively small.

At present, all sources of information concerning the national bibliography are incomplete, and none is organized in presentable form as such. However, events are on the move. The UPHU, which is actively attempting to secure Dominican Republic publications, is the institution which is listed as the contributor to the Caribbean Regional Library for *Current Caribbean Bibliography.* The Librería Hispaniola, an important bookstore in the capital city, is listed among the contributors to both *Fichero bibliográfico hispanoamericano* and to *Comentarios bibliográficos americanos.* The country is represented in the University of Florida Library's annual *Caribbean Acquisitions* to the extent that a standing LACAP order, exchange agreements, and miscellaneous sources provide materials that produce bibliographic entries. The quarterly listings in *Caribbean Studies'* "Current Bibliography" are regular, frequent, and the most extensive lists presently available.

A very promising factor in the situation is the news, contained on page one of the first issue of the UASD *Boletín de adquisiciones,* that strong reinforcements for the library world have recently been welcomed. Specifically, as of late 1959 five nationals (two men and three women) had just returned from the Escuela Interamericana de Bibliotecología, in Medellín, Colombia, newly equipped with their degrees in library science. The Director of the EIB, it will be remembered, is the Dr. Florén Lozano who, in the 1940s, had contributed to the Dominican Republic its first introduction to the type of organization which makes the difference between a mere assemblage of books and a library. Another new factor is that, in the neighboring island of Puerto Rico, a Graduate School of Library Science was inaugurated in 1969.

Summary

The Dominican Republic has had until now no regularly published and adequate records of its national book production. Such attempts as have been made to provide national bibliography are due to the efforts of a very few individuals who received their inspiration and training in the 1940s from a Spanish émigré, Dr. Luis Florén Lozano, and who have had to be responsible for all phases of library development in the country. The recent addition of graduates from the Interamerican Library School to the corps of professional librarians adds a new dimension to the possibilities for future progress. Representatives from the Dominican Republic have participated in recent Caribbean conferences. Prospects seem good for major advances, bibliographic and otherwise, in the 1970s.

HAITI

Haiti is another of the countries which owes most of its national bibliographic records to the efforts of one man—in this case, Max Bissainthe, formerly the Director of the National Library. Bissainthe's *Dictionnaire de bibliographie haïtienne,* covering from 1804 (the year when Haiti became independent of France) through 1949, was published by the Scarecrow Press in 1951 and was a tremendous boon to everyone at all interested in Haitian publications. Supplements covering one year or more at a time were published in *Conjonction: revue de l'Institut Français d'Haiti* from the early 1950s through 1965. In the May 1965 issue, "Bibliographie haïtienne pour les années 1962, 1963, 1964" brought the record up to date as of the mid-sixties. Soon after that time Mr. Bissainthe left Haiti for New York. While he does send out from there* occasional lists, he does not, of course, have full access to new Haitian publications, and few current titles are listed.

Haiti was represented at the ACURIL (Association of Caribbean University and Research Institute Libraries) Conference in San Juan, Puerto Rico, on June 14-16, 1969. However its only representation in the monthly *Supplements* to *Current Caribbean Bibliography* is by means of entries sent in from elsewhere, such as those supplied by the University of Florida Libraries, which are later included in their annual volume *Caribbean Acquisitions.* The most extensive current listings are those found in the quarterly issues of *Caribbean Studies,* in its "Current Bibliography" section.

During the life span of the *Bibliografía de Centroamérica y del Caribe,* Max Bissainthe had been the National Compiler for Haiti, sending his data to Fermín Peraza, the Technical Director. In what was, in a way, a natural extension of that relationship, Dr. Peraza completed during the last year of his life a compilation of available data on Haitian bibliography from 1950, the point where Max Bissainthe's *Dictionnaire* had left off, through 1967. His widow, Elena V. Peraza, stated in the final issue of their *Trimestre bibliográfico* (año 7/8, no. 26/27, oct./dic. 1968-enero/marzo 1969) that "Haitian Bibliography, 1950-1967," would be published by the University of Miami's Center for Advanced International Studies.

The chief direct source of publications from Haiti at present is the Librairie à la Caravelle, which sends out, very occasionally, lists of Haitian books for sale.† However, they ordinarily give only author, short title, date, and price. The Stechert-Hafner LACAP program can supply more materials than was the case until a year or so ago, but the coverage is by no means complete.

---

* Address: Max Bissainthe, 210 West 70th Street, Apt. 915, New York, New York 10023.

† When this author visited Haiti in October 1956 in search of Haitian materials and continuing sources for their supply, the proprietors of the Librarie à la Caravelle (P.O. Box 111, Port-au-Prince, Haiti) had just returned from Europe, where M. Max Bouchereau had served in a diplomatic post. He and his wife, Mme Madeliene G. (Sylvain) Bouchereau, were remodeling the bookstore. Plans were to devote one section to Haitian publications, to be presided over by Mme Bouchereau, a member of a leading Haitian family, who held a doctorate from a European university and was very knowledgeable about Haitian publications. To the best of my knowledge, the Bouchereaus continue to own and operate the bookstore. It has, of course, suffered in the series of misfortunes which has beset Haiti since that year.

Summary

With the departure of Max Bissainthe from Haiti, the country lost the immediate services of the one person to whom it is indebted for the existence of both a retrospective record from 1804-1949 and most of the data which made it possible for Fermín Peraza to compile a cumulated record from 1950-1967. At present, current bibliographical records are mainly dependent upon data supplied by institutions which specialize in the acquiring of Caribbean book materials from whatever sources are available to them.

THE ENGLISH-SPEAKING CARIBBEAN

Some indication of the increasingly active part the English-speaking Caribbean islands and Guyana have been playing in bibliographic developments during the past decade has already been made explicit in this study. Special attention was given to the beginning of active participation of representatives from the Caribbean at the Fifth Seminar, held at the New York Public Library in 1960. Their increasing participation since that time is at least implicit in the account so far given. The story is one to which full justice cannot be done within the scope of the present study, but a few particularly pertinent developments must be noted.

The sixties were a momentous decade for the area. The threshold of the seventies finds four newly independent English-speaking Caribbean countries—Jamaica (1962), Trinidad and Tobago (1962), Guyana (1966), and Barbados (1966). The fact that the three island countries have asked for and been admitted to membership in the Organization of American States does make them, if not a part of "Latin America," members of the family of nations composed predominantly of "Latin" countries but all of whose inhabitants are Americans. In terms of bibliography, a new national awareness had brought, appropriately, a desire to collect and publish the bibliographical record of the pre-independence period.

Jamaica, the oldest of the new nations (August 6, 1962), set the commendable precedent of publishing a selective national bibliography to celebrate its new status. *Jamaica: A Select Bibliography—1900-1963* was "compiled by the Jamaica Library Service and published by the Jamaica Independence Festival Committee in commemoration of the first Anniversary of the Independence of America." By "including the more important publications of the twentieth century dealing with all aspects of Jamaica," it attempted to portray the national heritage and the contemporary way of life. This excellent and attractively printed 115-page bibliography does credit to the Jamaica Festival Committee, whose financial assistance made its publication possible.

Barbados, which became independent in late 1966 (November 30), celebrated the event by preparing and publishing its first national bibliography: *Barbadiana: A List of Works Pertaining to the History of the Island of Barbados*. This 44-page multilithed bibliography, prepared and distributed by the Barbados Public Library, Bridgetown, in 1966 is a selective list of books and pamphlets from the colonial period to the present, but the term "history" is sufficiently inclusive to provide for sections on Government and Politics, Social and Economic History, and Education.

Guyana, formerly British Guiana, became independent on May 26, 1966. When it becomes a republic early in 1970, it will be the first of the non-Hispanic Caribbean countries to adopt this form of government. Its initial steps toward the compilation of national bibliography were taken in 1969. *A Selection of Documents on Guyana* was compiled by Claire Collins and Yvonne Stephenson of the University of Guyana Library for distribution to participants in the ACURIL Conference held in San Juan, Puerto Rico, on June 14-16, 1969. This 24-page mimeographed bibliography contains 429 items, of which some are 1968 and 1969 imprints. A preliminary version had been prepared as a contribution to the Conference on Sharing Caribbean Resources for Study and Research held on St. Thomas, Virgin Islands, March 17-19, 1969. It was welcomed there, but it was the interest and needs of the University's own community which led to the revision and expansion.

Trinidad and Tobago, which together became an independent nation on August 31, 1966, has not as yet produced a national bibliography. However the Central Library has for some time maintained a West Indian Reference Collection, which began to publish monthly a mimeographed *Classified List of Accessions* in 1965. In January 1966 (no. 39), the title was changed to *Trinidad and Tobago and West Indian Bibliography: Monthly Accessions*. Cumulated issues have been provided at irregular intervals. The first five covered 1965-1967 in periods of from four to six months. Cumulative issue number 6, however, covered all of 1968, and the preface indicated that future issues would continue to be on an annual basis. The cumulations have been presented as printed booklets, beginning with the third number, and they do have, of course, permanent reference value.

Mimeographed accession lists are prepared in all the major islands of the English-speaking Caribbean. They have traditionally served several purposes, notably to provide information to the local public about newly acquired materials and to serve as a medium of exchange regarding comparable data with exchange partners in the Caribbean or elsewhere. However, their usual arrangement is that of classification by subject, with no author index and without regard to time or place of publication. Their scope, if not general, is that of the "West Indies," which is fine on a regional basis but too inclusive to serve the purpose of national bibliography. Their chief value is ordinarily for immediate consultation for acquisition purposes rather than for long-term reference use.

A highly important element in the situation with respect to the English-speaking islands has been their growing sense of community interest in bibliographic developments as evidenced by the participation in such developments of their representatives during the past decade. Their contributions to SALALM have been important, but even more so has been their interest in the potentialities of the proposed Regional Bibliographic Center. It is hoped that, when and if they could, among them, develop their own acquisition procedures to the point of securing published materials and providing their corresponding bibliographic entries to an adequately funded Caribbean Regional Library for inclusion in its automated lists, their problems as to national bibliography would be well on the way to solution. Certainly it is in the interests of all concerned that procedures be developed to the point where the pressing of a key can produce an almost instantaneous printout of desired data, including selections by political units.

Meanwhile, for all the English-speaking units of the Caribbean area, one of the best single sources of current information concerning publications from or about them, including periodical articles, is the section, "Current Bibliography" in *Caribbean Studies*. In the cases of most of the Lesser Antilles this quarterly compilation, prepared under the direction of highly qualified librarians at the University of Puerto Rico's Central Library (which serves the UPR's Institute of Caribbean Studies), may well be practically the only source of current information about their individual islands.

General Summary for the Caribbean Area

In Central America the situation regarding national bibliography appears static. Costa Rica continues to be the only one of the six countries which consistently produces an annual record of the publications issued within its borders.

In Mexico, whose current bibliographic records are largely independent of the rest of the "Caribbean" area, recent developments provide that important country with both a reasonably current record and an excellent cumulated one.

Of the Caribbean islands, Cuba is the one with the longest and best bibliographic records. The tradition is being maintained under the Castro regime. Haiti, whose leading bibliographer has departed, provides no significant record of its current publications. In the Dominican Republic there are indications of interest, but there is as yet no publication which can be called a national bibliography.

It is in the islands with British and United States backgrounds that the most dynamic and promising developments are taking place. The intellectual climate, the professional education of librarians in the best universities of England and of the mainland United States, and their participation in national and international conferences have all contributed towards providing incentive and encouragement to improve the bibliographic records of their countries' publications.

The emergence of the Caribbean Regional Library in Hato Rey, Puerto Rico, as the focal point for the development of a current national bibliography on a regional basis represents a concentration of faith, hope, and knowledge, all crystallized by means of a great deal of cooperative effort. The Library, whose basic collection is a heritage from the Caribbean Commission (1946-1960) and the Caribbean Organization (1961-1965), is held in trust by the government of Puerto Rico until such time as a successor regional organization may come into being. It has been under the immediate jurisdiction of the Corporation for the Economic Development of the Caribbean, commonly known as CODECA (from the Spanish form of the title). Recent political changes in Puerto Rico have made the status of CODECA somewhat uncertain, but Commonwealth officials have given assurances of their desire to continue its support and of their intention to do so.

The Seminars for the Acquisition of Latin American Library Materials (SALALM) have provided moral encouragement, but little more, towards the development of a Regional Bibliographic Center in connection with the Caribbean Regional Library. Strong professional leadership, aided by financial support from CODECA sufficient to enable the CRL to employ topnotch professional assistance to develop suitable automated procedures, had brought the CRL by mid-1969 to a state of readiness to undertake service as a bibliographic center to serve the entire Caribbean area. The achieving of this "interim capability" stage for providing centralized bibliography for the Antilles was a major event in library development in the Caribbean area and was unmatched in the rest of Latin America.

The remaining need was for comparatively modest financial support. This was needed for two purposes: (1) to pay the costs, including some remuneration for the labor involved, of the collecting in the various islands of the data concerning their new publications and transmitting it to the CRL on the forms for use with automated MARC procedures and (2) the additional labor and production costs at the CRL. The result would be of tremendous benefit to the entire region and to all the political, commercial, cultural, and other entities interested in knowing what is being thought, done, and said in this area of vital concern to the Americas and of interest to much of the rest of the world. In tangible form it would be a bibliography compiled on a cooperative basis of publications in the region, with locations indicated. It would become increasingly comprehensive as the program gathered momentum. Publications about the islands as well as from them could be included as the situation warranted. For the individual islands, the programmed data could provide their national bibliographies at the touch of a button in accordance with the input that had been provided.

Meanwhile, a more conventional bibliography, one covering the Caribbean area, including the continental countries, is important both for itself and as a contribution towards the compilation of the Caribbean Regional Library. The University of Puerto Rico's Institute of Caribbean Studies (which has benefited from financial support provided by the Ford Foundation as well as the federal government) continues to supply up-to-date bibliographical information on a quarterly basis. The "Current Bibliography" section in its *Caribbean Studies* is an important source of information concerning publications of the islands and of the Central American countries. Since it is a subject bibliography, however, its listings of periodical articles and other materials may be, in some cases, largely or preponderantly nonnational in origin.

The financial investments of the Institute in the securing of the publications, in the salaries of the personnel who analyze and record the data, and in the publication costs of the results in its quarterly journal, *Caribbean Studies*, are considerable. The information serves an immediate purpose, but since it is noncumulative, the bibliography becomes cumbersome as a research tool. However, since the UPR contributes to the data provided by the Caribbean Regional Library's monthly *Supplements* to *Current Caribbean Bibliography*, to be cumulated annually, much of the information is in fact cumulated and so conserved for reference use and research.

At this point, even though the projected Bibliographical Center still awaits the support essential to its full development, it represents major achievements in at least two important respects. The monthly *Supplements,* which register publications received by the CRL and data supplied by contributing libraries, are being published by the most approved automated procedures. It was stated at the Fourteenth Seminar, which met in Puerto Rico in June 1969, that the 1969 volume of *Current Caribbean Bibliography* could be produced by the automatic compilation of the data from the monthly lists.*

Another major accomplishment of bibliographical endeavors in the Caribbean area has been the rather extraordinary one of developing regional cooperation among extremely diverse entities. A series of conferences of librarians, of which the first major one was in 1967, culminated in June 1969 in the organization of ACURIL, an association of Caribbean university and research institute librarians. The group is independent of SALALM but will cooperate with it and could possibly become an affiliate. The strength of the group centers in Puerto Rico and the English-speaking islands, but Haiti, the Dominican Republic, and the French and Dutch areas are cooperating actively. The circum-Caribbean area is initially represented by institutions in three states or countries—Florida, Mexico, and Colombia. A growing membership is anticipated.

The state of the art of current national bibliography in the Caribbean area is at a critical stage. A great deal has been accomplished. Far more is in sight. The future of a major and promising investment, centered in the Caribbean Regional Library and the potential Regional Bibliographic Center which is based there, depends upon events largely beyond the control of librarians and upon heaven-sent or other financial support.

* A form letter from CODECA, dated March 16, 1970, and signed by Olga Cuebas Vázquez, Acting Director of the Caribbean Regional Library, indicated that the December issue of the monthly supplements to *Current Caribbean Bibliography* had been distributed and that the 1969 cumulative annual should reach subscribers in mid-April.

APPENDIX

Seminars on the Acquisition of
Latin American Library Materials (SALALM)

There follows a list of the Seminars held from 1956 through 1969. Those for which *Final Reports and Working Papers* have been published by the Pan American Union in its "Reuniones bibliotecológicos" series are available from the Sales Division of the Pan American Union, Washington, D.C., 20006. For the others, copies of the pre-print working papers, as distributed to participants, are available from Microcard Editions, Inc., 901 Twenty-sixth Street, Washington, D.C. The institution named is that of the co-sponsor with the Pan American Union.

1st, University of Florida, Gainesville (held at Chinsegut Hill, Brooksville), June 14-15, 1956.

2nd, University of Texas, Austin, June 19-20, 1957.

3rd, University of California, Berkeley, July 10-11, 1958.

4th, Library of Congress, Washington, D.C., June 18-19, 1959.

5th, New York Public Library, New York, June 14-16, 1960. (Reuniones bibliotecológicos, No. 5.)

6th, Southern Illinois University, Carbondale, July 6-8, 1961.

7th, University of Miami, Coral Gables, Florida, June 14-16, 1962. (Reuniones bibliotecológicos, Nos. 1-2.)

8th, University of Wisconsin, Madison, July 11-12, 1963. (Reuniones bibliotecológicos, Nos. 3-4.)

119

9th, Washington University Library, St. Louis, June 25-26, 1964. (Reuniones bibliotecológicos, Nos. 6-7.)

10th, Wayne State University Library, Detroit, July 1-3, 1965. (Reuniones bibliotecológicos, Nos. 8-9.)

11th, Columbia University Libraries, New York, July 7-9, 1966. (Reuniones Bibliotecológicos, Nos. 12-13.)

12th, University of California at Los Angeles, June 22-24, 1967. (Reuniones bibliotecológicos, Nos. 14-15.)

13th, University of Kansas, Lawrence, June 20-22, 1968. (Reuniones bibliotecológicos, Nos. 16-17.)

14th, Caribbean Regional Library—CODECA and University of Puerto Rico, Río Piedras Campus, San Juan, June 17-20, 1969.

The Seminars on the Acquisition of Latin American Library Materials had their origin in a conversation of a small group of librarians who were discussing during a break at an American Library Association meeting, early in 1956, their problems in securing Latin American publications. It was agreed that the restructured ALA, which placed each program function in one of two categories—kind of library or kind of activity—offered no place to consider area programs. As a result, Stanley L. West, then Director of the University of Florida Libraries, and Marietta Daniels, Associate Director of the Columbus Memorial Library of the Pan American Union, agreed to ask their respective organizations to co-sponsor a meeting to solve these problems. Inasmuch as the ALA was to convene at Miami Beach in June 1956, it seemed appropriate to hold the proposed Seminar on the Acquisition of Latin American Library Materials in Florida immediately prior to ALA. The place was an estate, Chinsegut Hill, at Brooksville, Florida (between Gainesville and Miami), which had been left to the University of Florida by Colonel and Mrs. Raymond Robins.

Consequently, a limited group of about twenty representatives of libraries and the book trade met at Chinsegut Hill to discuss, and hopefully to settle, problems relating to (1) selection of materials and bibliographic sources, (2) book materials—purchase and exchange, (3) nonbook materials, (4) Latin American periodicals and their acquisition, (5) government publications and documents of inter-American organizations. Since the meeting, although profitable, failed to solve all problems, it was decided to accept a tentative invitation extended by Miss Nettie Lee Benson to hold a second Seminar at the University of Texas the following year, immediately preceding the annual ALA Conference in Kansas City. For that meeting a larger group could be invited, including library representatives from neighboring Mexico. Interest in increasingly defined problems and progress toward resolving at least one major problem—that of the indexing of Latin American periodicals—led to a decision to continue the Seminars. A resolution recommending that Miss Marietta Daniels be selected to serve as Permanent Secretary was adopted. An invitation from the University of California to hold the Third Seminar there, prior to the annual ALA Conference in Oakland in July 1958, was accepted. By then the need for continued Seminars and the precedent of holding them prior to the ALA Conference and more or less "in the general vicinity" were both established.

Bibliographies, when considered at all at the first Seminars, were treated exclusively as tools for acquisition purposes. It was not until the Fifth Seminar (1960) that it was recommended that a separate Committee on Bibliography be appointed, "to serve as an over-all committee for the various bibliographic activities and investigations of the Seminar." From then through the Tenth Seminar (1965), by which time all geographic areas had been covered, increased attention was given to bibliographic matters. An attempt was made to complete by then for each of the countries of Latin America the documentation in several matters—including the status of book publishing and of bibliography—which had been recognized as being complementary, if not interdependent.

Papers submitted for the Tenth Seminar left only Ecuador and Peru not covered by reports on bibliography, although for several countries of the Caribbean and Central America the only coverage had been that provided by Dr. Fermín Peraza at the Fifth Seminar in his paper "Bibliography in the Caribbean Area." A belated paper from Ecuador for the Eleventh Seminar (1966), "Apuntes bibliográficos," left only Peru unrepresented by a paper dealing specifically with bibliography.

In her introduction to the *Final Reports and Working Papers* of the Tenth Seminar, the Permanent Secretary, Mrs. Marietta Daniels Shepard, pointed out the changes that the decade had seen in the growth of Latin American studies in various countries. In the United States the growth was partially a result of the Alliance for Progress program, which considered education essential to social and economic development and which therefore encouraged studies in those fields on the part of persons who might render assistance. A change in the focus of the Seminars, toward library development programs in both American continents, was seen as desirable. At that point, however, it seemed well to consolidate gains before moving on. Two papers partially summarized accomplishments of the decade: "A Bibliography of Bibliographies of the First Ten Seminars," by Father Brendan Connolly and "Bibliographic Achievements of the Seminars," by Irene Zimmerman (Working Papers Nos. 5, 9).

The Eleventh Seminar considered for the first time the topics of Latin American collections, Latin American libraries, and the training of personnel for service in both. The shift of emphasis would avoid repetition of ground previously covered, while new bibliographic developments would be noted in the annual reports on that subject. At the final session the possible advantages of incorporating the Seminars, under the acronym of SALALM, were discussed. At the Twelfth Seminar a committee was named to develop plans for incorporation as a nonprofit organization, which would place SALALM in a position to accept government and foundation funds for its work and could make possible the wider distribution of the publications originating from its activities.

At the thirteenth meeting, in June 1968, it was reported that SALALM had become incorporated as a membership association of an educational character in January 1968. Officers were elected, and Mrs. Marietta Daniels Shepard was formally appointed Executive Secretary. At the Fourteenth Seminar, 1969, she reported that with the authorization of the Executive Board certain modifications in the Constitution and Articles of Incorporation had been made to meet requirements of the Internal Revenue Service for the granting of tax-exempt status and that the status had accordingly been granted on January 29, 1969.

The Fourteenth Seminar treated, as a special topic, scientific and technological materials from or about Latin America. In 1970 when ALA convenes in Detroit, SALALM is to meet in Canada, and in 1971, with ALA in Dallas, SALALM plans to meet in Mexico. The 1970 meeting is to give special attention to legal materials relating to social and economic growth. In 1971 the acquisitions and developmental problems of Latin American libraries will be considered. The Secretary states that beginning in 1972 more attention will be given to activities regarding Latin American acquisitions in Europe and other countries.

As evidenced by the summarizing papers at the Tenth Seminar, the attributable results of the Seminars in the United States are considerable. What the additional results may be is not subject to estimate. The same is true regarding results elsewhere, notably in South America. However, this writer found, in the course of her South American trip in the spring of 1969, that acquaintance with the Seminars in library circles was greater than she had anticipated. Certainly the interest of SALALM in national bibliography serves as a stimulating force in that respect, and its indirect influence should not be underestimated.

A SELECTIVE BIBLIOGRAPHY

1. Serials

Anuario bibliográfico. 1958- . México, Biblioteca Nacional, Instituto Bibliográfico Mexicano, 1967- .

Anuario bibliográfico colombiano Rubén Pérez Ortíz. 1951- . Bogotá, Instituto Caro y Cuervo, 1951- .

Anuario bibliográfico costarricense. 1956- . San José, Imprenta Nacional, 1958- .

Anuario bibliográfico guatemalteco. 1960. Guatemala City, Biblioteca Nacional, 1962/?

Anuario bibliográfico hondureño. 1961. Tegucigalpa, Editorial del Ministerio de Educación Pública, 1963.

Anuario bibliográfico peruano. 1943- . Lima, Biblioteca Nacional, 1945- . Irregular.

Anuario bibliográfico puertorriqueño. 1948- . Río Piedras, Biblioteca de la Universidad, 1948- . Irregular.

Anuario bibliográfico salvadoreño. 1952. San Salvador, Editorial Casa de la Cultura. 39 p. Anexo de *Anaqueles,* Época V, no. 4, 1954.

Anuario bibliográfico uruguayo. 1946-1949. Montevideo, Biblioteca Nacional, 1947-1951. 4 v.

Anuario bibliográfico venezolano. 1942- . Caracas, Tipografía Americana, 1944- . Irregular.

Anuario de la prensa chilena. 1877/85-1916, 1957/61- . Santiago de Chile, Biblioteca Nacional, 1887- . Irregular.

Atenea. v. 1- ; abril 1924- . Santiago de Chile, Imprenta Nascimiento, 1924- . Monthly.

BBB: Boletim bibliográfico brasileiro: revista dos editôres. 1952-1967. Rio de Janeiro, Sindicato Nacional das Empresas Editôras de Livros e Publicações Culturais, 1953-1968. Bimonthly; quarterly.

Bibliografía argentina de artes y letras. no. 1- ; 1959- . Buenos Aires, Fondo Nacional de las Artes, 1959- . Irregular.

Bibliografía boliviana. 1962- Cochabamba, Editorial Los Amigos del Libro, 1963- . Annual.

Bibliografía colombiana. v. 1-12; enero/junio 1961-1967. Coral Gables, Florida, 1961-1968. Semiannual.

Bibliografía cubana. v. 1- ; 1959/62- . Havana, Consejo Nacional de Cultura, 1967- . Irregular.

Bibliografía cubana. v. 1-29; 1937-1965. Havana; Gainesville, Florida, 1938-1966. Title varies: *Anuario bibliográfico cubano.* v. 1-16; 1937-1952.

Bibliografía de Centroamérica y del Caribe. 1956-1958. Havana, 1958-1960. 3 v.

Bibliografía de Centroamérica y del Caribe, Argentina y Venezuela. 1959. Havana, 1961. 438 p.

Bibliografía mexicana. no. 1- ; enero/febrero, 1967- . Biblioteca Nacional e Instituto Bibliográfico Mexicano, 1967- . Bimonthly.

Bibliografía oficial colombiana. no. 1- ; 1965- . Medellín, Escuela Interamericana de Bibliotecología, 1965. Irregular.

Bibliografía uruguaya. 1962-1963/? Montevideo, Poder Legislativo, Biblioteca, 1962-1963/?

Bibliographical Services Throughout the World: Annual Reports. 1st/2nd- ; 1951/53- . Paris, UNESCO, 1955- . Irregular.

Bibliography, Documentation, and Terminology. v. 1- ; March 1961- . Paris, UNESCO, 1961- . Bimonthly.

Biblio-notas. junio 1967- . Santo Domingo, Universidad Nacional Pedro Henríquez Ureña, Biblioteca, 1967- . Irregular.

Biblos: informativo bibliográfico. año 1-22; nos. 1-123. Buenos Aires, Cámara Argentina del Libro, 1941-1966.

Boletín bibliográfico ecuatoriano. v. 1; no. 1-2; enero/marzo–abril/junio, 1967. Quito, 1967.

Boletín bibliográfico mexicano. año 1- ; 31 enero 1940- . México, Porrúa Hermanos, 1940- . Bimonthly.

Boletín bibliográfico nacional. no. 1- ; enero 1937- . Buenos Aires, Dirección General de Cultura, 1937- . Irregular.

The Caribbean. v. 1-14. Port of Spain, Trinidad, Caribbean Commission, 1947-1960. Monthly.

Caribbean Bulletin. v. 1-6, no. 10. Río Piedras, Puerto Rico, University of Puerto Rico, Institute of Caribbean Studies, 1963-1969. Monthly.

Caribbean Educational Bulletin. v. 5, no. 11- ; September 1968- . Río Piedras, Puerto Rico, University of Puerto Rico, Institute of Caribbean Studies. 3 times a year. [Continues numbering of *Caribbean Bulletin.*]

Caribbean Journal of Science. v. 1- ; February 1961- . Mayagüez, Puerto Rico, University of Puerto Rico, 1961- . Quarterly.

Caribbean Studies. v. 1- ; April 1961- . Río Piedras, University of Puerto Rico, Institute of Caribbean Studies, 1961- . Quarterly.

Casa de la Cultura Ecuatoriana. *Revista.* v. 1-10; 1945-1957. Quito, Ecuador. Irregular.

Centro Latino-Americano de Pesquisas em Ciências Sociais. *Bibliografia.* v. 1- ; setembro/ outubro 1962- . Rio de Janeiro, 1962- . Bimonthly.

Comentarios bibliográficos americanos. no. 1- ; January/March 1969- . Montevideo, CBA Editores, 1969- . Bimonthly.

Conjonction: revue de l'Institut Français d'Haïti. no. 1- ; 1946- . Port-au-Prince, 1946- Irregular.

Costa Rica. Universidad Nacional, San Pedro. Biblioteca. *Lista de tesis de grado de la Universidad de Costa Rica.* 1957- . Annual.

Current Caribbean Bibliography. v. 1- ; June 1951- . Hato Rey, Puerto Rico, Caribbean Regional Library, 1951- . Irregular.

———. Supplement. January 1969- . Monthly.

Edições brasileiras: catálogo trimestral de livros publicados no Brasil. 1963-1966. Rio de Janeiro, Sindicato Nacional dos Editôres de Livros, 1963-1966. Irregular.

———. *Suplemento especial. Bibliografía brasileira de livros infantis.* Rio de Janeiro, Sindicato Nacional dos Editôres de Livros, 1968. 153 p.

Fichero bibliográfico hispanoamericano. v. 1- ; October 1961- . Buenos Aires, Bowker Editores Argentina, 1961- . Monthly.

Florida. University. Gainesville. Libraries. Technical Processes Department. *Caribbean Acquisitions: Materials Acquired by the University of Florida, 1957/58-* . 1959- . Annual.

Guatemala. Tipografía Nacional. *Catálogo general de libros, folletos y revistas editados en la Tipografía Nacional de Guatemala.* 1892- . Guatemala, 1944- . Irregular.

Guión literario. año 1- ; enero 1956- . San Salvador, Dirección General de Publicaciones del Ministerio de Educación, 1956- . Monthly.

Handbook of Latin American Studies. 1936- . Gainesville, University of Florida Press, 1937- . Annual.

Honduras rotaria. año 1- ; abril 1943- . Tegucigalpa, Honduras, Rotary Clubs of Honduras, 1943- . Monthly.

Indice bibliográfico de la Biblioteca nacional. no. 1-23; 1956-1965. Caracas, 1956-1965. Semiannual.

Indice bibliográfico guatemalteco. 1951-1960. Guatemala City, Instituto Guatemalteco-Americano, 1952-1960. 4 v.

Indice general de publicaciones periódicas latinoamericanas: humanidades y ciencias sociales. Index to Latin American Periodicals: Humanities and Social Sciences. Ed. by Jorge Grossmann. v. 1- ; 1961- . Metuchen, New Jersey, Scarecrow Press, 1962- . Quarterly.

Inter-American Review of Bibliography. v. 1- ; January/March 1951- . Washington, D.C., Pan American Union, 1951- . Quarterly.

Latin American Cooperative Acquisitions Project. *Latin America: Catalog.* no. 1 [no. 283 of Catalog]- ; 1960- . New York, Stechert-Hafner, 1960- . Irregular

Lima. Universidad Nacional de San Marcos. Biblioteca Central. *Boletín bibliográfico.* v. 1- ; 1923- . Lima, 1923- . Quarterly.

Managua. Biblioteca Americana de Nicaragua. *Bibliografía de trabajos publicados en Nicaragua.* 1943-1945/47. [Managua] 1944-1948. 3 v.

México. Biblioteca Nacional, México. *Boletín.* año 1- ; no. 1- ; 1904- . Quarterly.

Monthly News Service. 196? - . Buenos Aires, Fernando García Cambeiro, 196? - .

New Latin American Books: An Advance Checklist of Newly Published Titles Just Acquired Under the Latin American Cooperative Acquisitions Project (LACAP). no. 1- ; September 1962- . New York, Stechert-Hafner, 1962- .

Pan American Union. Columbus Memorial Library. *List of Books Accessioned and Periodical Articles Indexed for the Month of – ,* August, 1950? - . Monthly.

Peraza, Fermín. *Revolutionary Cuba: a Bibliographical Guide.* 1966-1968. Coral Gables, Florida, University of Miami Press, 1967-1969. 3 v.

Revista do livro. no. 1/2- ; junho 1956- . Rio de Janeiro, Instituto Nacional do Livro, 1956- . Quarterly.

Revista interamericana de bibliografía. SEE: *Inter-American Review of Bibliography.*

Rio de Janeiro. Biblioteca Nacional. *Boletim bibliográfico.* 1886; 1918; 1951- . Rio de Janeiro, Biblioteca Nacional, Divisão de Adquisição, 1886, 1918, 1951- . Semiannual.

Rio de Janeiro. Instituto Brasileiro de Bibliografia e Documentação. *Bibliografia brasileira de ciências sociais.* v. 1- ; 1954- . Rio de Janeiro [1955]. Annual.

Rio de Janeiro. Instituto Nacional do Livro. *Bibliografia brasileira.* 1938/39- . 1941- . Irregular.

Rio de Janeiro. Instituto Nacional do Livro. *Bibliografia brasileira mensal.* 1967- . 1967- . Monthly.

San José, Costa Rica. Biblioteca Nacional. *Boletín bibliográfico.* 1935/38-1955. San José, Imprenta Nacional, 1939-1956.

Santiago de Chile. Biblioteca Nacional. *Anuario de publicaciones periódicas chilenas.* 1937/38, 1952- . Santiago, Biblioteca Nacional, Dirección General de Bibliotecas, Archivos y Museos, 1937/38, 1952- . Annual.

Santo Domingo. Universidad. *Anales.* v. 1-26; enero 1937-1960. Quarterly.

Santo Domingo. Universidad. Biblioteca Central. *Boletín de adquisiciones.* September 1969- .
1969- . Bimonthly.
Servicio bibliográfico chileno. September 1940- . Santiago de Chile, Editorial Zamorano y
Caperán, 1940- . Quarterly.
Texas. University. Library. *Recent Acquisitions for Cuba of the Latin American Collection of
the University of Texas Library.* no. 1- ; 1962/March 1967- . Irregular.
Texas. University. Library. *Recent Acquisitions for the Caribbean Islands (excluding Cuba)
and Guyana, French Guiana and Surinam of the Latin American Collection of the Univer-
sity of Texas Library.* no. 1- ; 1962/March 1967- . Irregular.
Texas. University. Library. *Recent Acquisitions of Books, etc. from Central America by the
Latin American Collection.* no. 1- ; 1962/65- . Irregular.
Texas. University. Library. *Recent Brazilian Acquisitions, Latin American Collection, Univer-
sity of Texas.* no. 1- ; May 1963- . Irregular.
Texas. University. Library. *Recent Mexican Acquisitions of the Latin American Collection of
the University of Texas Library.* no. 1- ; 1962/64- . Irregular.
Trinidad and Tobago and West Indian Bibliography: Monthly Accessions. no. 1- ; September
1965- . Trinidad and Tobago, Central Library, 1965- . Monthly.
Venezuela. Biblioteca Nacional, Caracas. *Boletín.* 1923-1933, 1936, 1959-1960.

2. Books, Articles, and Papers

Abella, Rosa M.
   1966   "Publicaciones periódicas editadas en el exilio y en existencia en la Biblioteca de la
           Universidad de Miami." Seminar . . . 11th, New York. Working Paper No. 5. 22 p.
   1968   _____. Supplement. Seminar . . . 13th, Lawrence, Kansas. Working Paper No. 15.
           14 p.
   1969   _____. _____. Seminar . . . 14th, San Juan, Puerto Rico. Working Paper No. 4. 22 p.
Alvarado García, Ernesto, and others.
   1962   "The Booktrade, Bibliography, and Exchange of Publications in Honduras." Semi-
           nar . . . 7th, Coral Gables, Florida. Working Paper No. 12. 12 p.; annex, 21 p.
Alvear, Alfredo, and Ximena Espinosa.
   1966   "Ecuador, apuntes bibliográficos." Seminar . . . 11th, New York. Working Paper
           No. 6. 16 p.
Baa, Enid M.
   1960   "Inter-Library Cooperation and Its Relation to Problems of Acquisition of Library
           Materials from the Caribbean Islands." Seminar . . . 5th, New York. Working Paper
           No. 3. 19 p.
   1963   "Library and Bibliographic Activities in the Caribbean." Seminar . . . 8th, Madi-
           son, Wisconsin. Working Paper No. 10. 31 p.
      and Ligia Espinal de Hoetink.
   1964   "Library and Bibliographic Activities in the Dominican Republic." Seminar . . .
           9th, St. Louis. Working Paper No. 4. 32 p.
Barbados. Public Library.
   1966   *Barbadiana: A List of Works Pertaining to the History of the Island of Barbados.*
           Bridgetown. 44 p. Multilithed.
Benson, Nettie Lee.
   1960   "Report on the Latin American Cooperative Acquisitions Project." Seminar . . .
           5th, New York. Special Report No. 1. 20 p.
Berroa, Josefina.
   1961   *México bibliográfico, 1957-1960: catálogo general de libros impresos en México.*
           189 p.

"Bibliografía retrospectiva," por Microbius Bibliothecarius. IN: *Honduras rotaria* 26:244
1969 (marzo), 27-28.
Bissainthe, Max.
1951 *Dictionnaire de bibliographie haïtienne.* Washington, D.C., Scarecrow Press.
1052 p.
1965 "Bibliographie haïtienne pour les années 1962, 1963, 1964." IN: *Conjonction,* no.
98 (mai), 91-104.
Bixler, Paul.
1969 *The Mexican Library.* Metuchen, New Jersey, Scarecrow Press. 129 p.
Bohórquez, José Ignacio.
1966 "Lista alfabética de las entidades de la administración pública nacional de Colombia, 1821-1966." Seminar . . . 11th, New York. Working Paper No. 4. 8 p. + list,
125 p.
Breedlove, James McShane.
1964 "Library Resources and Acquisitions and Exchange Policies Relating to Peru."
Seminar . . . 9th, St. Louis. Working Paper No. 8A. 21 p.
Brennan, Mary.
1964 "Library Resources and Acquisitions [Paraguay]." Seminar . . . 9th, St. Louis.
Working Paper No. 8B. 16 p.
Casa de la Cultura Ecuatoriana.
1959 *Libros publicados por la Editorial de la Casa Matriz.* Quito, Ecuador. [13 p.]
1965 *Catálogo general de publicaciones de la Casa de la Cultura Ecuatoriana,*
1944-1965. Quito, Ecuador. 230 p.
Catálogo colectivo de publicaciones periódicas existentes en bibliotecas científicas y técnicas
1962 *argentinas.* 2d ed. Dirigido por Ernesto Gietz. Buenos Aires, Consejo Nacional de
Investigaciones Científicas y Técnicas. 1726 p.
Connolly, Brendan.
1965 "Bibliography of Bibliographies of the First Ten Seminars." Seminar . . . 10th,
Detroit. Working Paper No. 5. 14 p.
Conover, Helen F.
1960 "Records of Current Publishing in Latin America." IN: *Handbook of Latin Ameri-*
can Studies, vol. 22, 327-34.
Costa de la Torre, Arturo.
1966 *Catálogo de la bibliografía boliviana: libros y folletos, 1900-1963.* La Paz
[Editorial Universidad Mayor de San Andrés], 1966 [i.e., 1968] . 1255 p.
Couture de Troismonts, Roberto.
1965 "The Present State of Argentine Current National Bibliography." Seminar
. . . 10th, Detroit. Working Paper No. 12. 14 p.
Dardón Córdova, Gonzalo.
1962 "Four Topics Concerning Books in Guatemala." Seminar . . . 7th, Coral Gables,
Florida. Working Paper No. 11. 21 p.
Deal, Carl W.
1967 "Bibliographic Aids for Collecting Current Latin American Materials." Seminar . . . 12th, Los Angeles. Working Paper No. 22. 19 p.
Dobles Segreda, Luis.
1927-67 *Indice bibliográfico de Costa Rica.* San José, Costa Rica, Imprenta Lehmann. 11v.
Doria, Irene.
1964 "The Situation of Bibliography in Brazil." Seminar . . . 9th, St. Louis. Working
Paper No. 7. 13 p. + 3 appendices, 15 p.
Durón, Jorge Fidel.
1943 *Repertorio bibliográfico hondureño.* Tegucigalpa, Honduras, Imprenta Calderón.
68 p.
1946 *Indice de la bibliografía hondureña.* Tegucigalpa, Honduras, Imprenta Calderón.
211 p.

1961 "Los libros y publicaciones de 1960." IN: *Honduras rotaria* 18:206 (mayo/junio), 14, 31.

1968 "Libros y publicaciones de 1967." IN: *Honduras rotaria* 24:239 (febrero/abril), 5-10.

Easton, David K.
1960 "Patterns and Problems of Publishing in the Caribbean Area." Seminar . . . 5th, New York. Working Paper No. 5. 13 p.

El Salvador. Dirección General de Bibliotecas y Archivos.
1965 "Book Publishing in El Salvador." Seminar . . . 10th, Detroit. Working Paper No. 17. 21 p.

Fernández Esquivel, Rosa María.
1966 *Las publicaciones oficiales de México: guía de publicaciones periódicas y seriadas, 1937-1967.* México, Universidad Nacional Autónoma de México, Facultad de Filosofía y Letras. 269 p.

Ferraz, María Antonia.
1966 "Bibliografía brasileira." Seminar . . . 11th, New York. Working Paper No. 9. 11 p.

Garza, Peter de la.
1961 "Records of Current Publication in Bolivia, Ecuador, and Honduras." IN: *Handbook of Latin American Studies,* vol. 23, 408-13.

1963 "The Acquisition of Research Materials from Brazil and Their Selection." Seminar . . . 8th, Madison, Wisconsin. Working Paper No. 5. 15 p. + 2 appendices, 32 p.

Geoghegan, Abel Rodolfo.
1965 *Obras de referencia de América Latina.* Buenos Aires. 280 p.

Gocking, William E.
1960 "Exchange of Publications in the [British] West Indies." Seminar . . . 5th, New York. Working Paper No. 11. 12 p.

Grases, Pedro.
1961 "General Aspects of Bibliographic Activities in Venezuela." Seminar . . . 6th, Carbondale, Illinois. Working Paper No. 10. 12 p.

Gravenhorst, Hans.
1969 "El panorama bibliográfico documental en la Argentina." Seminar . . . 14th, San Juan, Puerto Rico. Working Paper No. 20. 8 p.

Gropp, Arthur E.
1968 *A Bibliography of Latin American Bibliographies.* Metuchen, New Jersey, Scarecrow Press. 515 p.

Handbook of Latin American Studies. Author Index. Nos. 1-28; 1936-1966. Gainesville,
1968 University of Florida Press. 421 p.

Herrera, Carmen D. de, and others.
1962 "The Booktrade, Bibliography, and Exchange of Publications in Panama." Seminar . . . 7th, Coral Gables, Florida. Working Paper No. 14. 14 p.

Jamaica. Library Service.
1963 *Jamaica: A Select Bibliography–1900-1963.* Jamaica Independence Festival Committee. 115 p.

Ker, Annita Melville.
1940 *Mexican Government Publications; A Guide to the More Important Publications of the National Government of Mexico, 1821-1936.* Washington, D.C., U.S. Government Printing Office. 333 p.

Kopper, Nelly.
1965 "The Booktrade in Costa Rica; the Present State of Costa Rican Bibliography; the State of Exchange in Costa Rica." Seminar . . . 10th, Detroit. Working Paper No. 14. 13 p.

Libros de Argentina: catálogo bibliográfico de la distribuidora Tres Américas. Buenos Aires.
1969 240 p.

Libros en venta en Hispanoamérica y España. New York, R. R. Bowker Co. 1891 p.
  1964
  1967   _____. Supplement, 1964-1966. Buenos Aires, Bowker Editores Argentina. 683 p.
  1969   _____ _____. 1967-1968. Buenos Aires, Bowker Editores Argentina. [Not yet seen.]
Maldonado de la Torre, Paulita.
  1967   "Considerations in the Development of a Caribbean Regional Collection." Semi-
          nar . . . 12th, Los Angeles. Working Paper No. 27. 9 p.
Mareski, Sofía.
  1964   "The Present Situation of Book Publication: Means of Production, Exchange of
          Publications, List of Official Organizations, and Bibliography of Official Publica-
          tions." Seminar . . . 9th, St. Louis. Working Paper No. 14. 4 p. + appendices, 6 p.
Matas, Blanca.
  1963   "Current Bibliography in Chile." Seminar . . . 8th, Madison, Wisconsin. Working
          Paper No. 13. 11 p.
Mendoza López, Margarita.
  1959   *Catálogo de publicaciones periódicas mexicanas.* México. 262 p.
Meneses, Marcela, and Werner Guttentag.
  1964   "Book Publishing in Bolivia." Seminar . . . 9th, St. Louis. Working Paper No. 10.
          34 p.
Mesa, Rosa Quintero, comp.
  1968a   *Latin American Serial Documents; A Holdings List: Colombia.* Ann Arbor, Univer-
          sity Microfilms-Xerox. 137 p.
  1968b   _____: *Brazil.* Ann Arbor, University Microfilms-Xerox. 343 p.
  1969   _____: *Cuba.* Ann Arbor, University Microfilms-Xerox. 207 p.
Mitchell, Eleanor.
  1968   "Pilot Project in the Andes." IN: *Library Journal* 93:20 (November 15), 4264-67.
Musso, Luis Alberto.
  1967   *Bibliografía del Poder Legislativo desde sus comienzos hasta el año 1965.* Monte-
          video, Uruguay, Cámara de Senadores. 236 p.
Peraza, Fermín.
  1960   "Bibliography in the Caribbean Area." Seminar . . . 5th, New York. Working Paper
          No. 7. 15 p.
  1964   *Publicaciones oficiales colombianas.* Gainesville, Florida. 31 p.
  1969   *Bibliografías corrientes de la América Latina.* Coral Gables, Florida. 75 l.
Pérez Ortiz, Rubén.
  1961   "Colombian Bibliography." Seminar . . . 6th, Carbondale, Illinois. Working Paper
          No. 14. 11 p.
Piñeiro, Miguel Ángel, and Luis Alberto Musso.
  1964   "Book Publishing in Uruguay." Seminar . . . 9th, St. Louis. Working Paper No. 13.
          10 p.
Ricketson, Edith B.
  1962   "The Acquisition of Research Materials from Central America and Panama and
          Their Selection." Seminar . . . 7th, Coral Gables, Florida. Working Paper No. 8.
          31 p.
Rio de Janeiro. Instituto Brasileiro de Bibliografia e Documentação.
  1968   *Periódicos brasileiros de cultura.* 2d ed. 280 p.
Sabor, Josefa E.
  1963   "La bibliografía general argentina en curso de publicación." IN: *Handbook of
          Latin American Studies,* vol. 25, 373-81.
  1967   *Manual de fuentes de información.* 2d ed. Buenos Aires, Kapelusz. 342 p.
San Salvador. Biblioteca Nacional.
  1956   *Bibliografía salvadoreña; lista preliminar por autores.* 430 l.
Savary, M. Jennifer.
  1968   *The Latin American Cooperative Acquisitions Program . . . an Imaginative Ven-
          ture.* New York, Hafner Publishing Co., Inc. 144 p.

Shepard, Marietta Daniels.
   1963   *An Inter-American Bibliographic Institute: A Proposal for Comprehensive International Bibliographic and Cataloging Control.* Washington, D.C., Pan American Union, Columbus Memorial Library. 12 p. (Cuadernos Bibliotecológicos, no. 16.)
   1968   "SALALM Progress Report, 1968." Seminar . . . 13th, Lawrence, Kansas. Working Paper No. 1. 89 p.
Summers Pagés, Bettina.
   1964   "The Publishing Industry in Peru." Seminar . . . 9th, St. Louis. Working Paper No. 12A. 3 p.
Turner, Mary C.
   1968   "Bibliografías corrientes de libros en nuestro idioma." IN: *Fichero bibliográfico hispanoamericano* 8:1 (October), 6 f.
U.S. Library of Congress.
   1945–   *A Guide to the Official Publications of the Other American Republics.* Washing-
   1949   ton, D.C. 19 v.
University of Guyana. Library.
   1969   *A Selection of Documents on Guyana.* Comp. by Claíre Collins and Yvonne Stephenson. Georgetown. 24 p.
Valenzuela Reyna, Gilberto, and others.
   1960–   *Bibliografía guatemalteca y catálogo general de libros, folletos, periódicos, revis-*
   1964   *tas, etc.* Guatemala, Tipografía Nacional. 10 v.
Vicentini, Abner L. Correa.
   1969   "The Organization of National Documentation and Information Services in Latin America with Special Reference to Brazil." IN: *Library Trends* 17:3 (January), 245-57.
White, Carl M.
   1969   *Mexico's Library and Information Services: A Study of Present Conditions and Needs.* Totawa, New Jersey, Bedminster Press. 106 p.
Zéndegui, Guillermo de.
   1964   "Temple of the Spanish Language." IN: *Américas* 16:1 (January), 4-9.
Zimmerman, Irene.
   1961   *Guide to Current Latin American Periodicals: Humanities and Social Sciences.* Gainesville, Florida, Kallman Publishing Co. 357 p.
   1965   "Bibliographic Achievements of the Seminars: Some Problems and Possible Solutions." Seminar . . . 10th, Detroit. Working Paper No. 9. 32 p.

INDEX